The Best Man Plays

Also by Andrew O'Toole

Branch Rickey in Pittsburgh: Baseball's Trailblazing General Manager for the Pirates, 1950–1955 (McFarland, 2000)

The Best Man Plays

Major League Baseball and the Black Athlete, 1901–2002

ANDREW O'TOOLE

McFarland & Company, Inc., Publishers
Jefferson, North Carolina, and London

LIBRARY OF CONGRESS CATALOGUING-IN-PUBLICATION DATA

O'Toole, Andrew.
The best man plays: major league baseball and the black athlete, 1901–2002 / Andrew O'Toole.
p. cm.
Includes bibliographical references and index.

ISBN 0-7864-1494-4 (softcover : 50# alkaline paper) ♾

1. Baseball players—United States—Biography.
2. African American baseball players—Biography.
3. Discrimination in sports—United Sates—History.
I. Title.
GV865.A1O86 2003 2003006889
796.357'64'08996073—dc21

British Library cataloguing data are available

Manufactured in the United States of America

McFarland & Company, Inc., Publishers
Box 611, Jefferson, North Carolina 28640
www.mcfarlandpub.com

For
Jaime and Courtney,
with love

One ever feels his two-ness— an American, a Negro; two souls,
two thoughts, two unreconciled strivings; two warring ideals
in one dark body, whose dogged strength alone
keeps it from being torn asunder.

W.E.B. Du Bois, *The Souls of Black Folk*

Acknowledgments

I would like to thank Bruce Markusen of the National Baseball Hall of Fame Research Center. Bruce not only offered encouragement for this project, but also thoughtfully provided me with valuable research material from the library's archives.

Thanks also to Linda Harper, Mel Moore, and Gary Mitchem for supplying much-needed criticism of the manuscript.

And lastly, my sounding board, my chief critic, my bride, Mickie. Though her name is not on the cover, this book is as much hers as it is mine. She is my muse, my love.

Contents

Preface: The Promised Land

Every man has the right to live
The right to a chance, to give what he has to give
The right to fight, for the things he believes
For the things that come to him in dreams
—Bruce Springsteen, "Follow That Dream"

Race has long been the defining, and dividing, issue in an America enamored of emphasizing differences among its citizens. There is enormous irony in the reality of a country that prides itself on being a "great melting pot" when more often than not it is a nation of self-imposed partitions. Be it social status, religious beliefs, ethnicity, sexual preference, or, most of all, race, the United States is a myriad of factions.

Sport, it's been said, is the great leveler. On the playing field all men are of equal status. Through the years few institutions have better embodied America's ideals— and prejudices— than baseball. For more than a century, the sport of baseball has proudly championed itself as America's "National Pastime." Not until April 15, 1947, however, did the game truly become democratic. On that spring afternoon Jack Roosevelt Robinson made his debut with the Brooklyn Dodgers. Robinson's appearance marked the first time an African American participated in a major-league contest during the twentieth century. Robinson's fiery style of play captured the imagination of his race, as his ability verified the truth of what many had believed all along: Blacks could compete on equal footing with white ballplayers, and excel ... *when given the opportunity.*

Baseball is integration, however, did not arrive without great struggle and debate. Arguments were put forth that Blacks lacked the necessary physical tools to compete with "big leaguers." Though lacking merit, such racism tinged arguments held sway for decades. Helped by the likes of baseball's first commissioner, Kenesaw Mountain Landis, and team owners such as Connie Mack, Tom Yawkey, and Walter Briggs, organized baseball remained staunchly segregated for nearly half the century. The game's leader and decision makers used their power to keep their intolerant belief system intact.

The prospects for integration had never been greater than in the years immediately following the conclusion of World War II. The death in 1944 of Landis, the most vehement and powerful opponent of integration, certainly contributed to the changing atmosphere. Another factor, the undeniable contribution made by African Americans in the war effort, should not be underestimated. Without a willing benefactor, however, these dynamics would have combined for naught.

Branch Rickey of the Brooklyn Dodgers would be the needed catalyst, Jackie Robinson his accomplice.

Robinson, however, is not the beginning of the tale. Scores of men, talented, ambitious, *deserving*, and Black, came before. Countless players of major-league caliber toiled in the Jim Crow Negro Leagues, their on-field exploits observed by a fortunate few. Tales of their genius, however, have been passed on through the years by those privileged to witness their feats.

Fleet Walker, Andrew Foster, John Henry Lloyd, Satchel Paige, Oscar Charleston, Cool Papa Bell, Judy Johnson.

Robinson's arrival certainly did not bring a halt to bigotry in professional baseball. Despite Jackie's undeniable success between the white lines, acceptance of Blacks in the big leagues was not soon forthcoming by many in baseball, both on the field and in the front offices throughout the league.

Baseball's integration served as a precursor to desegregation in everyday American life. Progress was slow, and acceptance begrudgingly given.

Larry Doby, Roy Campanella, Curt Flood, Henry Aaron, Willie Mays, Ernie Banks, Frank Robinson, Bob Gibson.

In a 1965 song, Otis Redding called for, and demanded, *Respect.* The soul artist captured a burgeoning sentiment among Black Americans; second-class citizenship, too long ingrained in the fabric of American society, would no longer be tolerated.

The growing Black pride movement found its way into the usually placid world of professional baseball. Traditionally, Black athletes were expected to be humble and obsequious. Those who were complacent about the inequitable status quo were considered a "credit to their race," while the outspoken Black athlete was considered a "race baiter" or a "clubhouse lawyer."

Curt Flood, among others, was vocal in his disapproval of baseball's antiquated policies. Led by Flood, the first generation of African American major leaguers were key participants in the growing Major League Player's Association. Power begets power, and power, of course, is fed by wealth. The rise of the MLPA allowed the empowerment of the Association's rank and file.

In short order, players found themselves on more a equitable footing with management. Decades of aristocratic rule by club owners had died an unceremonious death. In its wake came a new athlete. A more affluent, though less revered, athlete had arrived.

Jim Rice, Barry Larkin, Albert Belle, Barry Bonds, Kirby Puckett, Dave Winfield, Dave Parker, Eddie Murray.

The great financial revolution in sports, which germinated in the nineteen-sixties, prospered in the seventies and flourished in the eighties and nineties. The new distribution of wealth created a fresh dilemma for the game; the divergence between the paying customer and the performer had expanded with the rising salaries. Resentful fans struggled to comprehend how players could demand tens of millions of dollars to play a child's game. Even more, the public failed to appreciate, or sympathize with, the various labor squabbles that dotted the last quarter of the century.

The Best Man Plays makes no attempt to be a definitive history of baseball. The primary goal of this book is to communicate the experience of six African Americans as the game progressed, and as the country itself evolved into a truer representation of the promises it was founded upon. This volume studies a century of baseball told through the life stories of six individual men: Andrew "Rube" Foster, LeRoy "Satchel" Paige, Larry Doby, Curt Flood, Dave Parker and Barry Bonds. Each man, though remembered for his exemplary play on the field, was chosen to represent his era for reasons that transcend baseball ability.

Rube Foster was easily the most important figure in Black baseball during the first twenty-five years of the twentieth century. "The Father of Black Baseball," as Foster was called, excelled at every phase of the game he touched, including Hall of Fame—caliber pitching, Foster's foresight and initiative allowed future Black players to participate in (somewhat) organized leagues and to show their talents to a wider audience. This newfound exposure opened the door to debate on the possible integration of baseball's major leagues.

Satchel Paige enjoyed the benefits of Foster's organizing efforts. A phenomenal talent and extraordinary personality, Satchel captured the rapt attention of Black baseball's fans and press. Word of Paige's talent quickly reached the world of organized baseball, where an enchanted baseball press helped build Satchel into a near-mythical figure.

While Paige helped propel the prospect of integration with his brilliant pitching and engaging persona, he was not the first to be called when the major leagues decided to integrate. The enormous burden and notoriety that came with being the first Black in the majors was instead placed on the broad shoulders of Jackie Robinson. Just three months after Robinson's introduction, a 21-year-old native of Paterson, New Jersey, by the name of Larry Doby was asked to replicate Robinson's courageous feat with the Cleveland Indians of the American League. Although his arrival lacked the grandiosity of Robinson's debut, Doby successfully fulfilled his role as the first Black in the senior circuit, silencing critics of Branch Rickey's grand "experiment."

Curt Flood entered professional baseball with a naïve belief in the egalitarian spirit his country purportedly represented. He left the game hardened by the realities of his chosen profession's politics, and his nation's inherent bigotry. Flood is remembered less for his talent — which was exceptional — than for his role in challenging baseball's stagnant reserve clause. Curt's refusal to acquiesce when his team, the St. Louis Cardinals, traded him to the Philadelphia Phillies set in motion events that would lead to the financial emancipation of all major league baseball players.

Dave Parker wasn't the first to reap the benefits of Flood's battle; however, he was the first to reach the vaunted $1-million-a-year mark. Although he was the finest player of his generation, Dave's legacy is unfortunately tied to the Pittsburgh Drug Trial, in which he was a prominent witness. Parker's otherwise sterling career has been overshadowed by that infamous trial, which took place in the summer of 1985. Still, Dave found himself vilified in his hometown of Pittsburgh years before the drug trial took place. Evidence, circumstantial though it is, indicates that Parker's troubles can be traced to his race ... and his newfound riches, a combustible combination in the eyes of some ignoble bigots.

Barry Bonds has suffered much the same fate as Dave Parker. Bonds arrived in Pittsburgh three years after Parker left the city under a barrage of assorted refuse thrown from the stands of Three Rivers Stadium. Although Bonds sorely lacked the charming personality of Parker, he was easily Dave's equal on the field, possibly even surpassing his predecessor's exploits.

Bonds, perhaps more than any player of his era, represents the increasing chasm between players and fans. With the growth of new media outlets beginning in the mid-eighties, professional athletes found themselves scrutinized as never before. Sports talk-radio gave fans a forum never before offered in which to voice their displeasure; cable TV allowed access to game coverage from across the country; and the Internet made available sports pages from virtually every newspaper in the land. Such microscopic analysis was perceived by Barry Bonds as an encumbrance. He sometimes regarded the media as a biased medium, feeding the fury of bigoted fans that resented the great wealth garnered by players of color.

As the twenty-first century dawned, professional baseball players enjoyed wealth incomprehensible to the average fan. This financial prosperity did much to alleviate the innate bias still present in the game. Racial barriers certainly remain, as evidenced by baseball's inequitable hiring practices, but progress has undoubtedly been made over the years. Despite its failings, baseball was at the forefront of the civil rights movement, creating an atmosphere where equality, though sometimes slow in development, was accepted as a fundamental entitlement.

1

Now Is the Time: *Rube Foster*

Blackman!
What is in thy bosom? Pluck it
out — is it genius, is it talent
for something? Let's have it.

Marcus Garvey, 1934

Baseball existed before Rube Foster. Indeed, *Black* baseball was widely played before Foster first donned a pair of cleats and trotted onto a dust-covered diamond. Though the game was still in its infancy when Foster's playing career began in the latter days of the nineteenth century, baseball was already established as the National Pastime. Some three decades later, as his career and life came to a sudden halt, Foster would be eulogized as "The Father of Black Baseball."

Throughout the span of his career, Foster *was* Black baseball. Rube's interests and talents were wide ranging, and apparently effortlessly, he excelled, at nearly every facet of the game. First, he made a name for himself as a stellar pitcher; then he ventured into the art of field managing, where he was an innovative and imaginative bench commander. Foster's legacy, however, rests in his role as founder and administrator of the first viable Negro League.

Rube was Walter Johnson, John McGraw and Kenesaw Mountain Landis combined. He dominated every aspect of the game more than did any other participant in its history. "The only thing 'wrong' with Rube," a white operator commented, "was that he was colored. Otherwise, he would have been one of baseball's all-time great administrators."[1] While some viewed Foster's skin color as a deterrent, Rube wore his blackness as a badge of honor.

Rube's ability was matched only by his ambition. Foster's grandest vision, an all-Black league, came to fruition with the advent of the Negro National League. The league's motto, penned by Foster, summarized his credo: "*We Are the Ship, All Else the Sea.*"

As owner of the Chicago American Giants, Foster made certain that his charges did not feel inferior to their major-league counterparts. Foster outfitted his men with the finest equipment, paid competitive wages and transported his men in custom Pullman cars at a time when most Black teams wore ragtag uniforms and traveled in rundown buses. He instilled in his men the belief that they were "major league" in every sense but the title.

A "gentleman's agreement" among white administrators effectively forbade Blacks to participate in organized baseball. The prevailing bigotry of the day may have prevented Rube Foster from displaying his many talents in the major leagues; nonetheless, the imposing Texan left a lasting impression on the game. Be it as a player, manager, or league president, Foster was a leading light whose impact was felt long after he died at the youthful age of fifty.

Journalist Frank A. Young extolled Rube's influence simply and succinctly. "Rube Foster's name," he wrote, "is written in baseball history so deep that the years cannot erase it."[2]

I Fear Nobody

Andrew Foster was born on September 17, 1879, in the southwest Texas town of Calvert. Foster was named for his father, a presiding elder at Calvert Methodist Episcopal Church. The Reverend Foster impressed upon his son a puritanical belief system that the youngster would carry throughout his life. Unlike his father, however, the younger Foster discovered that the lure of the baseball diamond equaled that of the pulpit. Andrew faithfully attended services every Sunday, and religiously took to the sandlots following services.

Even at an early age Andrew a showed remarkable ability to organize and administer: While still in grade school he ran a team in his hometown. Foster quit attending the segregated Calvert school when only in the eighth grade.

At the age of seventeen Andrew left home and joined a traveling semipro club, the Waco Yellow Jackets. While the youngster may have lacked a formal education, he learned the difficult ways of the world by barnstorming through the Southwest. Years later Foster described the arduous lifestyle on the road: "[We] were banned away from homes ... as baseball and those who played it were considered as low and ungentlemanly.[3]" Finding lodging and food was never easy for a Black squad traveling through unfriendly territory. Foster, though, used his time spent with the Yellow Jackets as a stepping-stone to greater opportunity.

It was while Foster was a member of the Waco club that he first drew the attention of club owners from Northern cities. On one barnstorming trip the Yellow Jackets ventured to Hot Springs, Arkansas, where they met up with the American League's Philadelphia Athletics. Shortly after a standout performance against the Connie Mack–managed team, Foster was offered the chance to play with the Chicago Unions.

Andrew did not immediately leap to accept the Unions' offer. Instead, he played hard to get by insisting on a transportation allowance, a demand that was originally rejected. After some deliberation, though, the Unions' owner, Frank Leland, reconsidered. Leland would provide trainfare, but only after issuing Foster a warning. His club would be playing a rough schedule, Leland relayed in a wire to Andrew, including a number of talented white clubs ... would he be up for the challenge?

Foster, fresh off an impressive outing against one of the finest white clubs in baseball, replied with a plucky cable: "If you play the best clubs in the land, white clubs, as you say, it will be a case of Greek meeting Greek. *I fear nobody*."[4]

The burley, pistol-packing right-hander then accepted Leland's offer of $40 a month plus $.15 per meal, and in short order boarded a train bound for Chicago.

The beginnings of Foster's professional career are sketchy, as records were poorly kept if they were put to paper at all. Much of what passed through the years originated with the oral reminiscences of the men who played with and against Andrew. By all accounts, the brash twenty-four-year-old made an immediate impression. In his first start for Leland's club, Foster pitched a shutout. Over the next three months Andrew lost only one contest: however, he did not remain with Leland's team for long. While the Unions were barnstorming through Michigan, a disgruntled Foster jumped the teams and joined a white semi-pro club based in Otsego, Michigan.

Foster journeyed east following Otsego's season and joined the Cuban X Giants. "He depended on his windup and speed to win games," E.B. Lamar of the Cuban X Giants said. "Foster thought he knew more than anyone else and would take that giant windup with men on bases. They ran wild and that taught [him] a lesson. From then on he made a study of the game, and every chance he got he would go out to the big-league parks and watch the big clubs in action."[5]

Foster put his studies to practical use the following season. He had advanced past the stage of great unfulfilled potential and had developed into Black baseball's arguably finest mounds-man.

Foster led the X Giants to the 1903 "Colored Championship," winning four of the five Cuban victories in the series. The next year found him playing with the Philadelphia Giants, the Cubans' victims in the previous year's championship. It was while Foster was with the Philadelphia club that he earned the nickname that remained with him until his dying day.

"Rube" Foster was born on a summer afternoon in 1904, subsequent to Andrew's outstanding performance in a contest that pitted him against Rube Wadell. Wadell was widely considered one of the major league's prëeminent pitchers at the time, but Foster defeated him and his Philadelphia Athletics teammates, 5–2. Initially Andrew was christened "Rube beater," then the simpler "Rube" took hold.

Foster's triumph over Wadell was just one of a reported fifty-one victories he garnered during the '04 season. "Rube Foster," the *Chicago Inter-Ocean* commented, " is a pitcher with the tricks of an (Old Hoss) Radbourn, with the speed of an (Amos) Russie, and with the coolness and deliberation of a Cy Young. What does that make him? Why, the greatest pitcher in the country.[6]

"But," the newspaper added, "his color has kept him out of the big leagues, and that is why the Lelands and Philadelphia Giants have had the services of a pitcher who otherwise would be a priceless boon [to major league clubs]."[7]

The *Cleveland Post* was equally admiring of Rube's talent: "There have been but two real pitchers who have put their feet in the Cleveland ball yard," read the daily newspaper. "They are Addie Joss and Rube Foster."[8]

White baseball, while not allowing Rube to participate in league games, certainly did take notice of his skill. In the spring of 1903, John McGraw, the manager of the New York Giants, asked Foster to tutor two of his pitchers, Christy Mathewson and Joe McGinnity. McGraw had watched Rube perform on several occasions and found himself enamored of a key pitch in Foster's repertoire, the screwball. Foster's lessons paid immediate dividends for the New York duo. Mathewson leapt from 14 victories in 1902 to 34 in 1903. McGinnity, who won just eight contests in '02, jumped to 30 wins the following season.

Just as he gamely took on the opportunity to instruct the Giant hurlers, Rube also was more than happy to explain his pitching methods when asked. "I don't rely on any kind of ball," Foster explained. "I don't use any kind of system. I just size up the batter and give him what I think he can't hit. Sometimes it's a curve and sometimes it's a straight ball. And I can almost tell by instinct what's coming off behind me."[9]

Foster also authored a short piece for Sol White's *History of Colored Baseball*, offering prospective pitchers cogent advice. "The real test comes when you are pitching with men on bases," Foster wrote. "Do not worry. Try to appear jolly and unconcerned. I have smiled often with the bases full with two strikes and three balls on the batter. This seems to unnerve. In other instances, where the batter appears anxious to hit, waste little time on him and when you think he realizes his position and everybody yelling at him to hit it out, waste a few balls and try his nerve; the majority of times you will win out by drawing him into hitting at a wide one."[10]

Rube was known throughout Negro ball for impeccable control. "He could," one Blackball veteran claimed, "pick the buttons off your uniform one by one."[11]

Those who witnessed him in action never forgot the wonder of Rube Foster. Perhaps the finest player in organized ball wholeheartedly endorsed Foster's ability. "He's the smartest pitcher I have ever seen in all my years of baseball,"[12] Honus Wagner proclaimed.

In 1906 Rube revisited Chicago when Frank Leland hired him to manage his Giants. To insure a successful return to the Second City, Foster brought with him a number of Philadelphia Giant teammates. Relocating to Chicago were "Home Run" Johnson, Mike Moore, Bill Gatewood, Pete Hill, Bill

Rube Foster: "I fear nobody" (author's collection).

Bowman, Pete Booker, and Nate Harris. In addition to insisting that Leland take on the refugees, Foster was adamant that he release a number of Union Giants.

Foster's career as a dominant pitcher was relatively short. At the height of his powers Rube was the finest pitcher Black baseball had to offer, possibly the best in all the game. However, by 1907 Foster had become vulnerable on the mound; his 6' 4" frame, once solid as granite, had turned soft and flabby. His pitching prowess greatly diminished, Foster began to take to the mound only sporadically. Instead he concentrated his efforts on developing his managerial skills. Foster was a quick study at his new endeavor; his Giants were an immediate success, winning 110 of 120 contests, including a winning streak of forty-eight games.

Dave Malarcher, who would later star for Rube's American Giants, remembered the first time he saw Foster's club in action. "I never saw such a well-equipped ball club in my whole life," Malarcher said. "I was astounded. Everyday they came out in a different set of beautiful uniforms, all kinds of bats and balls, all the best kinds of equipment."[13]

Many of Foster's managerial stratagems were revolutionary; Rube was a mastermind at winning contests by mastering "inside baseball." It was often said that if an opponent walked a man against a Foster-managed club, it would cost that team a run. Rube's teams were expected to be masters at bat control. To play for Foster, a man was required to be able to bunt a ball into a cap ... literally. As a manager, Rube used these skills to great effect. One specific maneuver originated by Foster was the hit-and-run bunt.

The play was not complicated. With a speedster on first base, the batter would lay a bunt down the third base line. The runner would be off with the pitch and would not stop running as he approached second base. Third base would be left undefended as the third baseman charged toward the plate in order to field the bunt.

Should the third baseman stay back to guard the bag, the batter was assured a base hit. If he charged, the runner easily took third. Despite Foster's repeated successful use of the play, white baseball did not catch on, and the "bunt-and-run" was never attempted in the major leagues.

"The element of surprise in baseball is like everything else," Foster philosophized. "We do what the other fellow does not expect us to do."[14]

The exciting brand of baseball put on display by Rube's American Giants caught the eye of the white sporting press. "Recently, especially in games played in Chicago, the Negro teams have shown wonderful speed and skill in their work as well as remarkably good conduct," read a report in the *Sporting News:*

> They have developed the old happy-go-lucky high score games into regular aggressive, low scoring contests, with the same wonderful curve pitching, sharp calling of balls and strikes and superb throwing from both the in and the out fields that is evidenced in the regular games in the major leagues....
>
> Experts who have seen the Negro games in Chicago this year have been astonished at their wonderful progress and development, and now class some of the regular teams with the best there is in the regular major leagues.[15]

Just as he freely offered pitching tips to all who asked, Rube unreservedly dispensed his managerial philosophy to his players, some of whom later used his methods at the helms of their own clubs.

"One of the things Rube taught us was that you win the ball game in one or two innings, you don't win it over a long period," Dave Malarcher explained. "Once in a while, you'll see a game when they make one or two runs in the first inning, two more later, and so forth, but in most cases the game is won in one rally. That means when you get the opportunity to win it, you'd better win it now and not throw it away by doing the wrong thing."[16]

"*Now* is the time," Foster would implore of his charges. "You don't have to get three hits every day for me. You don't have to get even two. But I want them at the *right* time."[17]

"If you let a player make the pitcher pitch four and five balls to him, he will tire around seven innings," Foster offered, "and if you can hit him at the beginning you can hit him when he is weaker and less effective. It is at this point I always center my attack. In most cases it is successful. On the other hand, if you allow your players to make a few runs at the beginning of the game they become careless; should these few runs be overtaken they are in most cases beaten. That is why I vary my attack on the field."[18]

At times Rube's techniques bordered on the unconventional, but successful they proved to be none the less. The 1910 Giants, a club Rube later referred to as the best team he ever assembled, won 123 out of 129 games. John McGraw witnessed this edition of the American Giants in action. "If I had a bucket of whitewash that wouldn't wash off," the great Muggsy McGraw told his Black contemporary, "you wouldn't have five players left tomorrow."[19]

Bobby Williams, who played for Foster, described an exacting supervisor: "Oh Rube was strict; when he got angry with you, he got angry," Williams said. "I've seen him sit on the bench and somebody did something wrong—he smoked a pipe all the time—and he took his pipe and hit you on the head with it."[20]

Foster did not use his pipe solely as a blunt instrument. Occasionally Rube would signal his players with it from the bench. By holding the pipe at various angles, Foster could let his men know which play was on at the moment.

"Rube was a nice manager, an even tempered man," Floyd Gardner, another of Foster's underlings, remembered. "Rube never told me what to do after I left the ballpark. You can do what you want to do, but when you come to the ballpark he wanted you to play or he'd fine you."

"As long as I'm paying you," Foster was heard to say, "you'll do as I tell you."[21]

"Rube was a natural psychologist," Arthur Hardy said. "Now he didn't know what a psychologist was and he probably couldn't spell it, but he realized that he couldn't fraternize and still maintain discipline. He wasn't harsh, but he was strict. His dictums were not unreasonable, but if you broke one he'd clamp down on you. If he struck a fine on you, you paid, for there was no appeal from it. He was dictatorial in that sense."[22]

In 1909, a bitter in-fight between Foster and Leland led to a split between the two baseball innovators. Rube issued an ultimatum to his former mentor when he advised Leland that one of the two must go. But Leland was not intimidated, and did not back away from the club that he had nurtured to prominence.

Rube then went to Leland's financial backers, R.R. Jackson and Beauregard Mosely, and received their assistance for a new club. Ironically, after the split between the two men was made official, Foster rather than the team's originator retained the "Leland Giant" name. A Chicago Circuit Court made the unusual ruling allowing Rube to use the then-renowned appellation. Leland received only one concession from the court, the exclusive right to lease Auburn Park, the previous home of the Leland Giants.

Foster shrugged off the loss of the park as nothing more than a minor setback. Within days he had secured a lease for the use of Normal Park, a ball field located half a mile from Auburn Park. To insure himself a top-notch product, Foster looked eastward. Just a few months following his split with Leland, Foster raided the Philadelphia Giants. Among others, John Henry Lloyd and Bruce Petway were lured to his Leland Giants. Rube's club played under the name Leland Giants only for the 1910 season before changing their name to the Chicago American Giants; Foster envisioned his team as a prospective national outfit.

As his reputation grew, Rube became more vocal, and began to freely express his opinions on all matters concerning Negro baseball. High on Foster's list of concerns was the infiltration of whites into Black baseball. White ownership of Negro teams was a "dangerous predicament" threatening the heart of Blackball. Rube voiced his displeasure with this permeation often, and vowed to remedy the deplorable practice.

John Schorling, brother in-law to White Sox owner Charles Comiskey, proved to be an exception to Foster's own personal tenet. When Comiskey moved his club to new dwellings, an opening was created at South Side Park, the former home of the Sox. Acting as a front for Comiskey, Schorling formed a partnership of sorts with Foster. Schorling retained ownership of the park grounds while Rube held the title to the eight thousand-seat grandstands.

For the time being Foster forced himself to compromise his conviction of a completely Afro-centric enterprise, easing his self-imposed dictate for the sake of the time-honored motive: cash. Schorling's wealth provided Foster with much-needed economic backing, and though the collaboration can be seen as an example of hypocrisy by Rube, the partnership allowed Foster to build towards his goal of a true Race league. For the next decade Foster built the finest team in Negro ball and cultivated his own status among his peers. His American Giants traveled the countryside taking on all comers. Finally, during the winter of 1919, Rube attempted to form a Black league. In contrast to an aborted attempt at creating a league nine years earlier, Negro baseball was now graced by a better brand of businessmen. The prospects for a successful run had greatly increased.

Following the failure of that first Negro National League, Rube had become engaged in the "booking" of games throughout the midwest. Thanks to the enormous success of the American Giants, Foster had uncommon leverage. The American Giants would make use of many parks on a regular basis, while they would pass up the opportunity to perform in others because its occupants were not "booked" exclusively by Rube's agency.

This arrangement had wide-reaching ramifications which were not confined solely to Black clubs: Rube enforced this hard-line stance on all teams that visited Chicago, excluding major-league clubs.

As Foster's empire expanded, so did his imagination.

Born of Necessity

As the 1887 season opened, upwards of twenty Negro players were in organized baseball. The commingling of Black and white on the same playing field, though, was tolerated but far from accepted.

On July 19, 1887, Cap Anson, the game's most popular and powerful figure of the day, threatened to cancel his Chicago club's contest against Newark if Black pitcher George Stovey took the field for the opponents. Anson had previously attempted to intimidate an opposing ball club with a similar warning. His previous threat was directed at the Toledo club, which had Fleet Walker on its roster. The manager of the Toledo club, however, ignored Cap's warning and the Chicago manager relented. In 1887, though, Newark's bench coach acquiesced to Anson's threat creating an unfortunate precedent.

Anson's animosity toward the Black race was undeniable, as evidenced by his autobiography, *A Ball Player's Career*. In this memoir Anson referred to Clarence Duvall, an African American who served as the White Stockings' mascot, as a "chocolate covered coon," a "no-account nigger," and the "little donkey."[23]

Anson's bigotry nature certainly wasn't unique for his era. His position as the game's dominant figure, however, allowed for the implementation of his own personal bias. Adrian "Cap" Anson was the marquée player of the day. He joined the Chicago club in 1876 at the age of twenty-five and quickly established himself as one of baseball's finest players.

In 1886, at the advanced age of thirty-five, Anson had 147 RBI's and a record-setting 187 hits for the season. That year also saw the White Stockings' player/manager become the first man to collect 3,000 career hits. By the late 1880's Anson had evolved from baseball's best player in to its most influential voice.

Cap Anson (left) and Rube Foster (courtesy NoirTech Research, Inc.).

Following Anson's ultimatum, Newark dropped Stovey from its roster, which marked the beginning of the end of Blacks in organized ball. By 1889 Fleet Walker was the sole Negro left in the International League, and he existed in an increasingly hostile environment.

"He was the best catcher I ever worked with," Walker's teammate Tony Mullane said of Fleet, "but I disliked a Negro and whenever I had to pitch to him I used anything I wanted without looking at his signals."[24]

Walker played fifty games for Syracuse in 1889, his efforts amounting to just a .216 batting average. Fleet disappeared from baseball and went to work as a railroad clerk. With Walker's compulsory retirement Anson finally had his racially pure league.

"Blackball" was born as a necessary alternative. In the same vein as the advent of the Black press and the popularity of Race music and literature, Black baseball existed to satisfy the desires of a people excluded from the mainstream.

As the nineteenth century coalesced with the twentieth, Blackball was disorganized at best. Semi-pro and amateur clubs were formed throughout the country, yet the existing teams lacked a unifying presence. There was no league, thus no coherent schedule. Statistics were kept haphazardly at best, and the statistics that endured meant little because of the lack of commonality between club schedules.

The first Black professional team was organized in 1885. The Cuban Giants materialized as Negro players were finding access to white clubs drastically restricted. A reporter for *The Sporting News* testified to the quality of play among the Giants. "There are players among these colored men that are equal to any white players on the ball field," the paper's correspondent noted. "If you don't think so, go and see the Cuban Giants play. This club with its strongest players on the field would play a favorable game against such clubs as the New Yorks or Chicagos."[25]

The Giants were only the first of many Black organizations that quickly popped up across the country; the great majority of these teams were located in northern urban centers. Despite its progress, however, Negro baseball was a mere imitation of organized white ball at the turn of the century. Conversely, the more talented participants in Black baseball were equal to, and, in some cases, more talented than their white counterparts. The greatest of these players drew comparison to the finest in white ball. John Henry Lloyd was known as the "Black Wagner," in honor of Pittsburgh Pirate shortstop Honus Wagner. Jose Mendez became the "Black Matty" after Christy Mathewson, and Oscar Charleston was dubbed the "Black Ty Cobb." Though these nicknames may have been sorely lacking in imagination, they certainly illustrated the divergent worlds the men inhabited.

Several men of African American lineage attempted to make their way into organized ball near the turn of the century. These men hoped to "pass" by portraying themselves as American Indians, Cubans and sometimes Mexicans.

The most notorious example of such an attempt came in 1901, when Baltimore Orioles manager John McGraw tried to pass off Black second baseman Charlie Grant as a Native American named Chief Tokahoma. McGraw's scheme, like others similar in nature, never materialized. Ironically, Grant's opportunity was spoiled by the enthusiasm of Black fans who flocked to Baltimore exhibitions in the hopes of seeing "Tokahoma" perform. McGraw refused to test the "gentleman's agreement," and never tried to insert Grant into a regular-season game.

Following the Charlie Grant episode, the nearest a Negro would get to major-league competition would be in exhibition contests. During the first two decades of the century, Black and white clubs squared off against each other in a number of exhibition games before and after the major-league season. These contests continued fairly frequently until the 1920s, when Judge Kenesaw Mountain Landis entered the world of major league baseball.

With his electrifying mass of disorganized white hair and stern facial expressions, which perpetually articulated an apparent displeasure with the matter at hand, Landis took over as baseball's czar in 1920. The game's owners named the Judge as their commissioner in the wake of the Black Sox betting scandal, and Landis zealously took to his role as baseball's prëeminent authority.

Shortly after taking over the newly created position, Landis addressed the problem of the 1919 World Series betting scandal. Eight Chicago White Sox members admitted to the knowledge of, and in some cases, participation in, a conspiracy to fix the '19 Series between Chicago and the Cincinnati Reds. The bet, brokered by New York gangster Arnold Rothstein, and the scandal shook the game to its foundation. The game's powerbrokers hoped that by granting Judge Landis unbridled control, baseball's integrity would be secured.

In a sweeping decision, Landis cleaned up the Black Sox debris by banishing all participating members from the game for life regardless of their roles in the affair. The judge's broad dictum set the tone for his tenure as baseball's ruling commissioner. Landis freely imparted his wisdom, and in some cases his prejudices, in all his prominent decisions.

Though he had no official influence over Blackball, his decision-making sometimes affected Negro baseball's financial wellbeing. With some success, Landis sought to restrict the use of major league ball fields by

Negro teams. A blatant racist, Landis also hated to see major league clubs lose to Black teams in their occasional exhibition match-ups. To remedy that embarrassing state of affairs, the Judge limited the number of participating players from one white team. With this ruling Landis and organized ball could save face should a Black club defeat an opponent in a barnstorming competition ... after all, a Negro team hadn't defeated a white "team."

Legend tells of a meeting between the great Black ball czar and his white counterpart some time after Landis took office. Rube, the story goes, ventured to the Judge's office seeking permission for his league members to play in major league parks.

When he arrived at Landis's Chicago headquarters, Foster discovered that his reputation had preceded him.

"Why I know you!" the commissioner exclaimed. "You're Rube Foster."

During the course of their conference Foster questioned Landis about the commissioner's restriction of games between white and Black professionals.

"Mr. Foster," the Judge supposedly answered, "When you best our team it gives us a black eye."[26]

We Are the Ship ... All Else the Sea

"We have players who can bat and players who can field," David Wyatt wrote in the *Indianapolis Freeman.* "We have players who can pitch and who can run, we have magnates with the glad hand, also the baseball fan; we have coaches who can make a lot of fun. We have umpires, we have scribes, the latter to criticize; we have cranks and also enthusiasts; but of all this, the one we need most is the man who will say, 'Let's organize.'"[27]

Rube Foster heard the plea and answered the call.

At the turn of the twentieth century Blacks made up just 2 percent of Chicago's population. Thanks to the industrial boom of the century's first two decades, the African American population in northern urban centers mushroomed. Foster recognized the potential of a greatly enhanced customer base and decided to act.

"Organization is its (Blackball's) only hope," he said. "With the proper organization, patterned after the men who have made baseball a success, we will, in three years, be rated as other leagues are rated."

"It would be such a crime," he added, "for the Negro who has such an abundance of talent in such a progressive age, to sit idly by and see his race forever doomed from America's greatest and foremost sport."[28]

For Black baseball to flourish, Foster understood that it was imperative to rein in the independent nature of the game. Player raids and contract jumping were rampant in the sport. For Black owners to maximize profits they must combine their resources under one roof. On February 14, 1920, Rube presided over a two-day meeting held at the YMCA in Kansas City. Representatives of the Detroit Stars, the Indianapolis ABC's, the Kansas City Monarchs, the Chicago Giants, St. Louis Giants and Dayton Marcos were all in attendance. Also in Kansas City for the groundbreaking gathering were several sports writers, there to record the historic affair.

Foster, representing the American Giants and the Cuban Stars, proposed a bold initiative: another Negro National League. In establishing a new NNL, Foster hoped "to create a profession that would equal the earning capacity of any other profession," and "to keep Colored baseball from the control of whites ... [to] do something concrete for the loyalty of the race."[29] The NNL, though unstable, proved to be an archetype of Black self-reliance. (Rube did, however, relent slightly in his wish for an all-Black league. J.L. Wilkinson of Kansas City was the sole white owner among the NNL's eight-team membership.)

A constitution was drawn up by the attendees at the Kansas City meeting. Each member franchise was forbidden to raid the rosters of agreeing teams, fines would be implemented for ungentlemanly conduct on or off the field, and contract jumping by players was banned.

The constitution bound all teams to play when and where Foster commanded. Also included in the league charter was a clause stating that all balls, bats and uniforms must be purchased from Rube, who in turn bought the equipment wholesale from Spaulding.

Journalist Al Monroe explained the process. "If eight thousand balls were purchased," Monroe wrote, "that meant one thousand for each club which were shipped at the opening of the training season. If some owners needed less than that number the "overs" were the owners' property as they were charged up with the balls."[30] Foster, of course, received a kick back from the supplier in return for providing such a large contract.

As self-appointed league president, Rube drew no salary. He did, however, garner 10 percent of the gate for each league game. Foster justified this hijacking as payment for his role as the league's booking agent. It was reported that Rube garnered $11,220 in 1920 alone from this revenue.

Rube also understood the need for competitive balance among league teams. Using his czar-like powers, Rube occasionally shuffled players from one team to another in order to maintain a semblance of equality. Rube even went so far as to transfer Oscar Charleston, perhaps the league's best player, from his own American Giants to the Indianapolis ABC's.

Though Rube occasionally took advantage of his powerful position as league president, he could also be a benevolent ruler. There were many reported instances of Foster using his own money to assist both players and teams in need. During the winter months Rube would sometimes advance pay to players beset with financial difficulties. "It will be August before that fellow pays me back all the money I have advanced him, but I guess he has to live,"[31] Foster was heard to say.

Foster was very generous when compensating his players as well. In 1923 his lowest paid man earned $175 a month, an excellent wage for Negro players of the era. He was also known to grant his players season-ending bonuses. The more capable players received as much as $3,000 in supplemental income.

In addition, Rube bailed out NNL clubs that ran into pecuniary trouble. Foster's financial aide kept the Dayton franchise afloat. When the Marcos still couldn't survive in the Gem City despite the influx of Foster's cash, they relocated to Toledo at the league president's expense. The club faltered again in Toledo. This failure could be attributed in large part to the fact that Foster couldn't properly oversee the operation.

On a number of occasions, Foster wired money to teams that had run out of funds while on the road. Furthermore, he routinely advanced cash to clubs struggling to meet their payrolls. Though some viewed Foster as a munificent leader, he certainly wasn't lacking critics. His antagonists viewed Rube's domineering tactics as dogmatic.

"Many a time have I sat in his office and observed him direct managers in other cities of the league as to the proper pitchers to assign to certain games,"[32] journalist Al Monroe reported of Rube's dictates. While seen today as an absolute conflict of interest, it *was* in the best interests of the league. Foster believed it was vital to the league welfare to maintain a competitive balance among teams. By manip-

Rube Foster, the "father of Black baseball" (author's collection).

ulating starting pitchers, among other things, Foster sought to sustain equality (to some extent) between league clubs.

"He didn't believe in beating anybody bad," Rube's younger brother Bill explained. "It would draw the crowd away. If you can win the ball game, win it, but don't best the other team so bad that nobody wants to see the team the next time it comes (to town)."[33]

Several more Black leagues sprouted up following the birth of the NNL. The Eastern Colored League came soon after the founding of the Southern Negro League. These new leagues were not bound to adhere to the NNL constitution and in time Eastern teams were raiding National clubs.

In contrast to the virtual all-Black ownership of NNL clubs, white businessmen backed a number of teams in the Eastern circuit. Among ECL owners, only Alex Pompez of the Cuban Giants and Ed Bolden of the Philadelphia Hilldales were Black. Rube looked upon his counterparts with contempt. "Calling the ECL 'Black,'" Foster said, "was like calling a streetcar a steamship."[34]

"Had the great Mogul used his organizing genius toward perfecting a league," a critic wrote, "success would have come to the project, but an outfit constructed for personal gain, however beneficial during its run, must tumble when the main link drops out."[35]

The "main link" was in reference to the mental collapse of Rube Foster.

"Rube had a fine mind," Dave Malarcher remembered. "As an owner, as a manager, he used to come in the clubhouse in the spring of the year, and I marveled at the mind that he had. He was president of the league, owned our team, and [managed] our team, even though he was the biggest man in baseball ... But I guess he wore himself out. He broke himself down."[36]

Rube's breakdown came suddenly and with little warning, though there were disturbing hints of the affliction that was to come. Willie Powell, a member of the American Giants, claimed to have seen Foster shagging imaginary fly balls outside his Michigan Avenue home. On another occasion Rube barricaded himself in a washroom, and one of his players had to crawl through a window to coax Rube out of the room. There were other, similar tales, which document Foster's rapidly deteriorating mental health; however, no concrete diagnosis was ever offered explain his illness.

"What his trouble was I don't know, but he was off and he never did get back to normal," Earl Foster, Rube's son, remembered. "It could have been a borderline case. He wasn't dangerous or anything like that, but he couldn't be at home. Sometimes he'd recognize you and sometimes he wouldn't."[37]

"The night he went crazy we were sitting upstairs and his wife hollered, 'Oh no, don't do that!'" George Sweatt relayed. "So I ran down and knocked on the door. I said, 'Mrs. Foster, is there something wrong with Rube?' 'He's just going crazy down here. I'm going to have to call the law.'"[38]

The police were called and when they arrived it took a handful of men to subdue the deranged Foster. Baseball's greatest mind suddenly and sadly gave out. Rube was remanded to an asylum for the mentally ill by judicial ruling in 1926. The final four years of his remarkable life were spent in a Kankakee hospital, where he roamed in and out of lucidity.

On December 9, 1930, Rube Foster's fertile mind was silenced forever.

Rollo Wilson eulogized Foster in the pages of *The Pittsburgh Courier*: "When the big game shall have become history there will stalk across the pages of the record a massive figure and its name will be Andrew Foster," Wilson wrote. "A loud-voiced man with a smelly pipe who kids his opponents and makes them like it. The dominant power of the commission and of the league. The master of the show who moves the figures on his checkerboard at will. The smooth-toned counselor of infinite wisdom and sober thought. The king who to suit his purpose, assumes the robes of his jester. Always the center of any crowd, the magnet attracting both the brains and the froth of humanity. Cold in refusals, warm in assent. Known to everybody, knows everybody. That's Rube."[39]

Black baseball did not forget its greatest benefactor. Huge floral arrangements were sent to Rube's funeral from leading men in the world of Negro ball. The Negro National League directors sent a huge 200-pound arrangement of chrysanthemums in the shape of a baseball. The American Giants Booster Association offered a large baseball diamond with Rube's initials placed in the center of the arrangement, with crossed bats and a baseball above. Chicago's Black community came out en mass to pay its respects. Several thousand were among the funeral congregation and thousands more viewed the body of the fallen hero.

Fittingly, as reported by *The Chicago Defender*, the casket was closed at "the usual hour a ballgame ends."[40]

The Negro National League faltered while Foster languished in the Kankakee asylum. Though the league would survive a couple of years after Foster passed on, Joe Green, owner of the Chicago Giants, acknowledged, "When Rube died, the league died with him."[41]

Despite the relatively short existence of the Negro National League, the groundwork had been laid. From its ashes would rise new Black associations, molded in the image of Foster's groundbreaking effort. The ensuing leagues played in better facilities, traveled in higher style and dressed in finer attire than their predecessors; but they lacked the defining presence of Rube Foster. Though the Negro Leagues were actually made necessary by segregation, Foster elevated the game to a *higher* level. "In keeping with the times," Foster insisted, "do something concrete for the loyalty of the Race."[42]

2

Satch the Sage: *Satchel Paige*

Customarily, myths are born in time. An occasion can arise, though, when spirit, ability and personality culminate in a living, breathing legend. In the case of LeRoy "Satchel" Paige, all necessary factors entwined leaving in their wake a wondrous combination of truths, tall tales, exaggeration, and fact. The beautiful and enduring story of Satchel Paige began in an America entrenched in racial segregation, and persisted, with great hesitation and reservation, as the country and his profession, became integrated.

His baseball career became the stuff of folklore, and Satchel never failed to enrich his own life story when conversing with interested parties. Paige's narrative begins in Mobile, Alabama, in the year of "who knows when."

"I pocketed my first dime by haulin' satchels in the Mobile railroad depot," Paige explained in his first autobiography, *Pitchin' Man*. "When the train chooed in, us kids would dash for the satchels, grab what we could and carry them to the depot."[1]

An enterprising lad, young LeRoy displayed an early thirst for cash that would remain with him:

"I got to thinkin', 'one satchel, one dime. Two satchels, two dimes, three satchels, three dimes ... the more satchels, the more dimes.' I needed more hands.

"So I got me some strings, swung them around my neck, shoulders and waist and tied satchels to 'em. On a good trip I could string up sixteen satchels, put one under each arm and two in each arm and two in my hands. A two-dollar payload.

"When I was full-up, the kids couldn't see me 'cause I was

Satchel Paige with the Monarchs (author's collection).

camouflaged like a moving satchel tree. After that they called me 'Satchel'."[2]

While there may be truth in Paige's effervescent account, one biographer speculated that Satchel acquired his renowned nickname from the youthful offense of luggage theft. Each explanation is plausible, and conceivably the biographer's telling rings truer, after all, Paige did spend part of his adolescence in reform school. But only a curmudgeon would allow the facts to stifle an exceptional anecdote.

Satchel's upbringing, embellished as it may have been, was fairly representative of a generation of African Americans. LeRoy was the seventh of eleven children brought up by Lula and John Paige in a four-room "shotgun" house. "Four rooms can get awful crowded," LeRoy would later recall.

"We had a pretty rough gang down on the South Side of Mobile, near the bay, where I was born and raised. We were exclusive, that's the word. When the South Side gave a picnic, the North Side couldn't come. They always tried, for sure. But we chased them right back.

"Fact is," Paige freely admitted, " we stoned them back with bricks. We had the best sham battlin' crew in Mobile Bay and I was known as the straightest brick thrower in Mobile."[3]

Paige would later insist that he learned his famous "hesitation" pitch from this childish mischief. "If a man was throwing at you, you couldn't just stand there, you'd duck. But if a man started to throw, and you ducked, and then he stopped, where would you be? Why you'd be standing there duckin', with your bare face, ready to be bangoed big as you please.

"Knocked a few fellows unconscious, but nothing serious. I know there's lotsa heads runnin' round Mobile right now that I helped raise. When I stang those fellows then, they didn't like me nohow."[4]

Hurling stones metamorphosed into heaving baseballs in competition. The cheers Paige heard while kicking around the sandlots of Mobile were intoxicating. Semipro ball, however, is not where fortunes lie. Money, Paige reckoned, equaled freedom and peace of mind.

"You just keep scratching and trying to get a dollar," Satch allowed. "Sometimes you do and sometimes you don't. Sometimes you forget you get hungry. Sometimes you forget how you can't buy clothes. Sometimes you forget, but usually you don't.

"I didn't forget and the more times I remembered how poor I was, the more I wanted to have something better. And the only way I knew how to get something better was pitching. That meant I had to get a professional ball club interested in me."[5]

While performing for the semipro Down the Bay Boys, Satch ran up a twenty-five game winning streak and professional baseball did come calling. Midway through the 1926 season the Chattanooga Black Lookouts of the Negro Southern League invited Satchel to the professional ranks. On May 16, 1926, Paige pitched his first pro game, against the Memphis Red Sox. For a teenager leaving Mobile for the first time, the monthly pay of $250 was a fortune. (Two hundred was sent home to his mother, and LeRoy kept fifty for himself). And Satchel discovered he was a soul born for the road. *"If you keep movin', Ol' Age ain't got a chance of catching you. He moves slow."*[6]

Following a successful stay in Chattanooga, Alex Herman, the owner of the Black Lookouts, sold Paige to Birmingham of Rube Foster's NNL. The conversion to the "big" leagues translated into a hike in pay ... for Lula Paige. "It meant $450 a month, $400 to Ma and the same $50 to me. All I was eatin' anyway those days was ice cream 'n cake and you sure could buy an awful lot o' that for $50.... Fact is, I was the sweetest man in Birmingham."[7]

Two years at Birmingham and Satchel was on the move again. This time his destination was Nashville, where he would perform with the Elite Giants. A habitual practice of jumping from team to team, of "followin' that buck wherever it did show," began for Paige at this time. From Nashville, to Cleveland, to Baltimore, Satchel followed the highest offer for his services. As the rest of the country fell into the Great Depression, Paige's fortunes continued to rise. "Like most people, I won't forget 1929. 'Course most will remember it because that's the year Ol' Satch's stock just started going up and up."[8]

Money certainly motivated Paige, but one aspect of the good life still eluded him: fame. To capture the celebrity he so desired, Satch trained his sights on the Pittsburgh Crawfords, "The highest of the high, the cream."[9]

Baseball on the Hill

With Rube Foster gone, baseball's Black leagues lacked focus. The cohesion that Foster had nurtured through the twenties soon dissipated. By 1931, Foster's Negro National League was out of business and the future of Black baseball seemed bleak. Into this languishing enterprise came William "Gus" Greenlee.

Greenlee was an underworld character of some note in Pittsburgh's Hill District who, admittedly, knew little about the game of baseball. Such inconsequential deterrent as a lack of knowledge never slowed a man of great ambition like Greenlee, however.

Gus entered the business of baseball in 1930 when he bought a sandlot club named the Pittsburgh Crawfords. Greenlee outfitted his troops in uniforms promoting James J. Coyne for Allegheny County commissioner. His primary purpose in buying and building a baseball club originally centered on promoting his political cronies and laundering his ill-gotten gains. Before long, though, Gus was caught up in the potential of his new purchase and gradually constructed a team that became the envy of all Black baseball.

During the 1931 season, Greenlee made the first of these transactions, one that moved his team into the pantheon of all-time great baseball clubs. In the disorderly world of Negro baseball contracts the agreements were acknowledged, but frequently violated. By simply offering more cash, Gus plucked Satchel Paige from the roster of the Cleveland Cubs, defying a standing agreement between Paige and the Cubs. "With the Crawfords I got fame and a heavy load of greenbacks,"[10] Paige reported.

Satch made his Crawford debut on August 6, 1931, against their crosstown rivals, the Homestead Grays. Paige entered the contest in the fourth inning with the Craws up 8–7. The final tally had Greenlee's boys victorious 11–7, and Satchel was credited with the win. "When I kicked up my foot and threw that first one, the crowd screamed," he remembered. "I kept kicking that foot up in the sky, twisting like a pretzel, pushing and throwing. I beat the Grays without any trouble and struck out sixteen to boot."[11]

With the goal of erecting a world-class ball club, Gus added another star to his stable following the '31 season when he stole hometown wunderkind Josh Gibson from the Grays. Then Oscar Charleston joined Paige and Gibson on the Crawfords. The trio formed the nucleus of a first-class franchise; all they needed was a home for this powerful club. Awaiting the Craws for the opening of the 1932 season was the first Black owned ballpark, Greenlee Field.

Located at 2500 Bedford Avenue on the Hill, Greenlee Field sat 7500 and was built at a cost of $100,000. The significance of Greenlee's proprietorship is vast, as Negro team owners had long been at the mercy of the whites that owned the ballparks. Gus recognized the need for Black ownership when he experienced the struggle of trying to secure a field. Contests were scheduled around the needs of major league tenants, often leaving Black clubs with less desirable dates

There were also indignities included with such arrangements. For instance, Cum Posey's Grays were permitted to rent Forbes Field from the Pittsburgh Pirates, but the Homestead nine were forced to shower and dress at a local YMCA because the Pirates would not open their clubhouses to the Grays. With Greenlee Field, Gus's club would not be forced to face such ignominy, not, at least, when they were playing at their home on the Hill.

The inaugural contest at Greenlee's new playpen pitted the Crawfords against the New York Black Yankees. Paige took to the mound for the Craws in front of a capacity crowd. Satchel came out on top 1–0 while tossing a six-hitter with ten strikeouts.

Greenlee Field was a great success. The yard would host a number of different events, including football, soccer, and prizefights. The ballpark saw 119,000 paid admissions stroll through its gates during its initial year. Following events at the park, sporting fans could patronize another Greenlee venture, the Crawford Grille. Located on Wylie Avenue in the Hill District, the two-story cabaret and restaurant was widely known for its great food and even better musical shows. In its heyday the nightspot was a Mecca for Black entertainment, playing host to a number of brilliant acts. Duke Ellington, Billie Holiday, Count Basie, and Cab Calloway were just a few of the many immortal artists who graced the Grille's stage. Greenlee, albeit a man of dubious character, recognized the power intrinsic in the belief in self-worth and racial amour proper. At his Crawford Grille, sport met culture. The renaissance of Black art was in full bloom and Greenlee, unsavory reputation and all, was doing his part to promote Black pride.

Leading into the '32 season Greenlee set out to resurrect the Negro National League, which had lain dormant since Rube Foster's incapacity and subsequent death. For his dream of resuscitating the league to become a reality, Gus would need an infusion of cash. Not surprisingly, Greenlee turned to his associates in the underworld. The gangsters, already heroes to some degree in their neighborhoods, relished the opportunity to launder their income from illegal activities in the guise of baseball revenue.

Joining Greenlee in the world of Negro league baseball was a varied conglomeration of second tier hoodlums, most of whom made their boodle from the numbers racket while more powerful white gangsters looked down upon such two-bit operations. Alex Pompez, owner of the Cuban Stars and protégé of Dutch Schultz, ran the numbers in Harlem. The owner of Newark's Eagles, Abe Manley, was a numbers banker in Camden, New Jersey. Even the well-respected, legitimate businessman Cum Posey was eventually forced to turn to the underworld when his Homestead Grays were financially strapped. Posey enlisted Rufus "Sonnyman" Jackson to help keep his club afloat. Jackson, a rival of Greenlee, earned his way with a variety of illegal endeavors and was more than willing to use the occasion to cleanse his gambling profits.

The reorganized NNL helped provide Black outfits with a measure of security, both financial and political. The teams now worked (for the most part) in concert for the betterment of Black baseball. Following the first season of the reinvented NNL, Greenlee spawned another idea that brought the circuit some much-needed positive exposure. The East-West Classic, Greenlee's spin-off of major league baseball's newly established All-Star game, offered the league and its players a day in the sun.

Through ballots placed in the nation's leading Black newspapers, most prominently the *Chicago Defender* and the *Pittsburgh Courier*, fans chose the participants in the Classic. The minority populace, long excluded from the nation's polls, took this balloting very seriously. Because the *Defender* and the *Courier* were the largest Black papers in the country, players from Pittsburgh and Chicago dominated the East-West squads. This glitch in the balloting process did not dampen the enthusiasm for the event. The East-West battle served no small part of an emerging Black consciousness, a feeling that was expanded upon by *Courier* reporter Mal Goode.

"There was so much negative living that we had to do over which we had no control," Goode explained. "You must remember that you didn't go into the bank and see a Black teller in those days. You didn't see a Black man driving a streetcar. Anything that we could hang onto from the standpoint of pride."[12]

The East-West Classic was an event; it quickly became *the* event for

Black America. Ticket sales were brisk for the first Classic. Train cars full of fans from as far away as Arkansas, Georgia, and Kansas arrived in Chicago with a final destination of Comiskey Park on their itinerary. The 1933 contest, held on September 10, drew just 20,000 but the event grew over the ensuing decade as its social significance expanded in Black culture. Upwards of 50,000 fans would attend the annual event at Chicago's south side park in the coming years.

For a period of time, it seemed as if everything Gus Greenlee touched turned to gold. His image as "Mr. Big" in Black Pittsburgh was firmly established as the Depression intensified its grip on the country. Gus's significance went beyond his role as a gangster or baseball owner; more importantly, he became a public benefactor who used his power and profits to improve living conditions on the Hill.

Greenlee promoted Black enterprise in Pittsburgh by giving a number of interest-free loans to Black business owners who were denied credit by white-run banks. Gus also expressed his largess by contributing to several charities and organizations whose missions were to improve the quality of life for Black Pittsburgh.

Beyond social concerns, Greenlee tried to treat his players "first class." His Crawford teams were among the finest in Negro baseball, some would even argue that the best Crawford teams were on a par with the best teams in the American and National circuits. Cool Papa Bell, Ted Page, Jimmy Crutchfield, and Judy Johnson joined Paige, Charleston, and Gibson on the Craws. These men, with five future Hall of Famers among them, formed the nucleus of the 1935 Crawford club, a team depicted by many as "the Black New York Yankees."

Greenlee outfitted these greats in the finest uniforms, had them travel in style in a custom made Mack bus and provided a palace in which his team performed their heroics. Gus's munificence to his players was not limited to their time spent in uniform; he often Greenlee made it a practice to care for his players in the off season. Judy Johnson was once paid to serve as Gus's paid chauffeur on a trip to Chicago. Ted Page, on vacation from his duties as a Crawford fly chaser, spent one winter as a paid "lookout" while Greenlee and his henchmen counted each day's take inside the Grille.

"They gave me a chair, my job was to sit downstairs on the sidewalk and ring a bell," Page told baseball historian John Holway. "Anybody who was coming in who wasn't supposed to be there, I would just push a button to alert them upstairs to get rid of all that money. That's all I did."[13]

By offering his players such jobs, Greenlee provided the men with much needed off-season income, and more importantly, earned their loyalty. However, loyalty, especially in Blackball, was as fleeting as next year's contract offer.

Player fidelity to Greenlee remained relatively secure for a short while. The roof caved in, though, in 1937, when Rafael Trujillio enticed a number of Black stars south to Santo Domingo, where they played for his national team. With suitcases full of cash, the Dominican dictator lured a virtual all-star team to his country. Paige, with his status as baseball's best pitcher and gate attraction, was greatly coveted by Trujillo.

"In 1937," Satchel later recounted, "most of those checks was being waved by teams down in the islands, and there was a whole flock of boys jumping Negro league contracts and heading down that way. I wasn't the only player around who did some fast stepping in those days, and you better believe it."[14]

The increase in pay certainly helped entice the Black stars to forsake the Negro Leagues, but it was more than the lure of cash that took the players south. "I didn't quit Newark and join some other team in the United States," shortstop Willie Wells wrote in the *Pittsburgh Courier* following his defection from the NNL. "I left the country. I found freedom and democracy here. Something I never found in the United States ... here I am a man."[15]

Satchel and Josh Gibson, among many others, followed the scent of freedom (and cash), to the Dominican Republic. These men stayed just one year, during which Paige and Gibson led the Trujillo All-Stars to a league title. Though the men found social conditions more tolerable in the Dominican Republic, they did not relish playing ball for a dictator who had armed troops at his disposal. During the championship game, troops flanked the perimeter of the playing field, rifles at the ready, should the All-Stars fail in their endeavor. Fortunately, Paige and his teammates were able to eke out a victory and did not have to face the wrath of Trujillio.

In reneging on his Crawford agreement, Paige continued his ignoble proclivity for not honoring contractual obligations. Following his one-year sojourn, though, Greenlee attempted to lure Paige back into the Crawford fold with an offer of $350 a month, roughly fifty percent less than Satchel's last contract with the Crawfords. The right-hander dismissed the overture out of hand. "I wouldn't throw ice cubes for that kind of money,"[16] he declared, with more than a hint of pomposity.

Fed up with Paige, Greenlee, who still considered the right-hander his "property," attempted to sell Satch's contract to the Newark Eagles for $5,000, only to have the deal nullified by a non-compliant Paige. "*He was selling a piece of paper and not the real stuff.*" Satchel related.[17]

Outraged at being stiffed by Paige again, Greenlee became intent on using his powers to keep Satch from playing for any of his competitors. Satchel was to be, "banned forever from baseball."[18] The banishment did not faze Paige one iota. Instead of sulking, he packed his bags and again headed south. This time Mexico was his destination, where Jorge Pasquel agreed to compensate him at an astonishing $2,000 a month.

Satchel's stay in Mexico was not a glorious one. In fact, the legend of Satchel Paige ended south of the border when his right arm suddenly lost its wonder. Inexplicably, Paige's pitching arm became a source of great pain, reaching the point where Satchel couldn't even lift it, let alone cut loose with a fastball. Clearly not the player he had been, Paige struggled through the Mexican League season. When the year came to a close, Pasquel was no longer interested in retaining Paige's services, a turn in fortune that left a bad taste in Satchel's mouth. "Once you couldn't make them any money," he moaned, "they didn't care about you."[19]

Paige sensed none of the irony that flowed through his words. Surely, in his eyes, leaving Greenlee after Gus had made him the highest paid performer in Black baseball was just good business. With the shoe on the other foot Paige saw no fairness in the act.

His right "flipper" now aching and virtually useless, Satchel's worst fear was that he would have to leave baseball and return to Mobile. "It'd been a long time since I'd thought about having nothing, about how it was to grow up in Mobile," Satchel later related in *Maybe I'll Pitch Forever*. "Ten years can make for a lot of forgetting. Now I started remembering. I didn't want to go back, but baseball was the only thing that'd keep me away."[20]

Mobile, and the life it represented to Paige, couldn't have been further from the world he had built for himself in the previous decade. To maintain that lifestyle, or at the very least a remnant of it, Paige turned to J.P. Wilkerson the owner of the Kansas City Monarchs, and practically begged for a spot on the club.

Wilkerson, cognizant of Satchel's ailing arm, nevertheless recognized the marquee value Paige's name still possessed. Instead of hiring him for the Monarchs, Wilkerson suggested that Satch join one of Kansas City's satellite teams. Satchel's role on the barnstorming club would be as a pitcher, but solely as a gate allure. The scheme hatched by Wilkerson had Paige's duties limited to playing first base, or perhaps just standing in a coach's box. The outfit would be dubbed "Satchel Paige's All-Stars."

"I'd been dead," Satch said. "Now I was alive again. I didn't have an arm, but I didn't even think of that ... I had me a piece of work."[21]

The All-Stars were a great financial success. Attendance at their exhibition contests was even higher than at most NNL games. Paige's legend had grown so great that fans flocked to see him even though his was just an honorary position on the squad. Then, remarkably, almost as quickly as he'd lost his fastball, he got it back.

Seven months of inactivity helped strengthen Satch's weak pitching limb. The rendition of his recovery that Paige translated to writer Richard Donovan in 1953 may resemble the truth, but one mustn't forget Satch's propensity for exaggeration, especially if it would enhance a tale.

As Paige told it, prior to a Monarch game a warm-up toss went past its intended receiver. Satch ambled over, picked up the ball, and flung it to a teammate.

"Walking thoughtfully toward the dugout," Donovan wrote. "Paige picked up a glove and called for a ball. Without a word, the Monarchs catcher left the plate and stationed himself about pitching distance from Paige. Then Paige began to throw, easily at first, then harder and harder. Nobody moved, the stands were silent, the game waiting. Then, abruptly, he stopped, and gazed around at all the eyes upon him.

"'Well,' he said, 'I'm back.'"[22]

Again able to pitch, Satchel relinquished his first base duties and took to the hill. The Monarchs' traveling team continued traversing the Northwest, stopping in "every town we could find."[23] This was a lifestyle Paige and his Blackball brethren had learned to live with. League teams, too, were often forced into this nomad existence by the promise of much-needed cash influx that came from such barnstorming tours. Uneven league scheduling allowed clubs to line up contests against a variety of opponents. Semi-pro teams, local nines, and aggregations of white college players all pitted their wares against the best of the Negro Leagues.

Barnstorming was the lifeblood of Black baseball teams. More often than not, the additional income from these non-league contests helped keep many teams afloat. Though these contests took place throughout the country during the summer months, a great majority of the off-season barnstorming trips took place down South through backwoods towns. Seemingly every Black player from the pre Civil Rights era came equipped with scores of anecdotes that aid in documenting a disturbing facet in American history.

Cool Papa Bell, for example, remembered one particular encounter when the Crawfords were traveling through Mississippi in Greenlee's custom-made bus. "We stopped at a colored restaurant in the little town of Piscayne, Mississippi, and tried to get something to eat," Bell recounted.

"'Oh no,' said the people at the restaurant. 'There are too many of you. It'll take us too long to fix food for so many.'"

"The restaurant people came out and looked at our bus, and one of them said, 'Who's on this bus? Any white boys on it?"

"'No,' we told them."

"'Who owns it?'

"'The Pittsburgh Crawford baseball team. Can't you read the sign?'

"'A colored baseball team?'

"'Well,' they said, 'you better get out of Mississippi as quick as you can.'

"'Why?'

"'Because if you don't, they're going to take all you guys on this bus and put you working out on the farm.'

"'Who's going to put us on a farm?'

"'The police, that's who. There's a lot of people out there on the farm right now they caught passing through. They jail people for speeding and then make them serve their sentence out on the farm. They love to catch colored folks.'

"Well we got back on the bus right away. We drove straight through until we were out of the state of Mississippi. It's a good thing Satchel wasn't with us. He always traveled in his own car, you know. If he had been with us, there would have been trouble. Satchel was not a man to take racial things without fighting back. He would have challenged somebody."[24]

Two of Bell's Crawford teammates, Judy Johnson and Ted Page, encountered their own surreal experience in the Deep South. "There were two guys," Johnson said, "and they told us they didn't like the way we were dressed. We were dressed pretty well, of course, and they said they didn't want any 'high falutin' niggers in our town.' They told us to get out or they'd shoot us.

"Once in a while the people would get mad when we beat their boys." Johnson continued. "Sometimes it got really nasty. Once, they stopped the Crawfords' bus on the way out of town and charged the driver with running a red light and speeding. He hadn't done either, but the team secretary had to pay a big fine before we could leave town."[25]

More often than not, Satchel traveled in his own vehicle, separate from his teammates. A Black man traveling through the American South in an expensive automobile was, to say the least, conspicuous, making Paige an easy target for overzealous police officers. A favorite story among former Negro Leaguers was of one such encounter Satchel had with Southern jurisprudence.

"One time Satchel got picked up for speeding," Judy Johnson explained. "Knowing Satchel, he probably was speeding. Anyway, he went up before the local judge and was fined forty dollars. Satch gave the judge eighty dollars and told him he was coming through again the next day."[26]

Despite constant encounters with racism, the men who beat the bushes in search of a game and a dollar spoke fondly of their barnstorming days. Their common experience served as a bond for the men in trying times. Their shared passion for the game of baseball was stronger than the distractions and slights they encountered on their travels.

"On the bus people slept, ate, kidded around, sometimes sang, and spent a lot of time discussing baseball," Cool Papa related. "We all loved the game and we had great pride in ourselves. We always wanted to do better and one of the best ways to get better is to discuss your mistakes and get advice from the other guys. We all pulled together and tried to help each other. I guess doing well was so important to us because we wanted to prove to the white man that we were good enough to play in the major leagues."[27]

Organized ball, and its unofficial ban on players of color, limited the Negro players' chances of proving their ability firsthand. Black players had to satisfy themselves with the rare opportunity of playing white major leaguers on the exhibition circuit. For a period of time in the twenties, Black clubs would play major-league clubs in post-season exhibition contests. Judge Landis, fearing that continual success of Negro teams against intact major league teams would put undue pressure on him to allow Blacks to participate in organized ball, banned complete teams from participating in these contests. For white professionals to barnstorm against Blacks, they had to be part of an "all-star" aggregate.

"They was keeping Blacks out of the Major Leagues, and if we could beat 'em, why not let 'em play? So they would let 'em play as an All-Star team, and if we beat 'em, we hadn't beat no big league team."[28] Cool Papa reasoned.

Thanks to Judge Landis, the best of the Negro Leagues were never to be pitted against the best of the major leagues. All future interracial competition would be contested with a diluted white club, which was usually made up of one marquee name, several respectable major leaguers, and a handful of semipro players. The main attraction at these contests, of course, was Paige. The biggest crowds turned out when Satchel was pitted against the best draw the major leagues had to offer in the early thirties, pitcher Dizzy Dean.

The two were, in many respects, mirror images of one other. Dean and Paige dominated the Depression era in a way none of their ball-playing contemporaries did. On the hill, Dean was as dominant as Paige, and Dizzy, a down-home spirit who hailed from Arkansas, could be as unrestrained and unpredictable away from the mound as Satchel. Like Satch, Diz occasionally struggled to fulfill his contractual obligations. Beyond the irresponsible side of their personalities, similarities between the two were persistent.

Paige and Dean both spewed fire from their right arms. Together, and apart, they attracted tremendous crowds to the ball orchard to witness their physical brilliance, and amused America with their verbose wit and charm.

Dean displayed his prolixity and pomposity prior to the 1934 season when he told reporters what to expect from him and his younger brother in the upcoming campaign. "Me-n'-Paul are gonna have a family contest," Dean proclaimed. "If I win more games than he does, I'll lead the league. And if Paul wins more games than me, I'll run second. I don't see how anybody can beat us Redbirds now with two Deans on the ballclub. We'll be sure to win 45 games between us and if we have six more pitchers who can win about 50 other games that will put us in the World Series. It ought to be a breeze from here on."[29]

The Brothers Dean delivered on Dizzy's promise and then some, with the elder sibling ringing up thirty wins while Paul chipped in an additional nineteen victories. (Their teammates won an additional forty-six.) Their Cardinal club, buoyed by the pugnacious duo, won the world championship when St. Louis defeated the Detroit Tigers in an action packed seven-game Series.

Following that title-capped season, Dean took a team of "All Stars" barnstorming throughout the countryside, where they competed against a number of semi-pro teams and occasionally a Negro-league club. In the fall of '34, Dean's All-Stars met up with Satchel and the Pittsburgh Crawfords. All who witnessed the occasion would long remember the ensuing contest. Baseball executive Bill Veeck was in attendance that afternoon and claimed that the game was "the best I've ever seen."[30]

Dizzy held the powerful Crawford club to just a single run while striking out fifteen, while Satch shut out Dean's assemblage while fanning seventeen. The two great hurlers would match up on numerous occasions through the ensuing years. These repeated surveys of Satchel's skill made a deep and lasting impression on Dean.

"A bunch of fellows get in a barber session the other day and they start to argue about the best pitcher they've ever seen," Dean stated before rattling off a litany of past baseball stars. "Some say Lefty Grove and Lefty Gomez and Walter Johnson and old Pete Alexander and Dazzy Vance. And they mention Lonnie Warneke and Van Mungo and Carl Hubbel and Johnny Corrider tells us about Matty and he sure must have been great and some of the boys even say Old Diz is the best they've ever seen. But I see all them fellows but Matty and Johnson and I know who's the best pitcher I've ever seen and its old Satchel Paige, that big lanky colored boy."[31]

Diz, in a fit of uncharacteristic modesty, continued, "Say, Old Diz was pretty fast back in 1933 and 1934, and you know my fastball looks like a change of pace alongside that little pistol bullet old Satchel shoots up to the plate."[32]

Dean then acknowledged the obvious, yet unspoken, truth about major league baseball, as he lamented the absence of great Black players from big-league squads. Considered more than six decades later, more than a half-century following the integration of the major leagues, Dean's words lose some of their pungency. At the time of Dean's bold proclamation, however, baseball vehemently denied the existence of any official ban on Black participants, and here was one of the game's great stars endorsing the ability of a Black player. Unfortunately, Dizzy's statement was not widely reported. Such quotes were usually confined to the Black press, where they would be heralded, while all but ignored in the mainstream media.

Throughout the thirties and forties the dilemma of segregated baseball was largely ignored in traditional media outlets; that is, the white-edited newspapers. The press, in their silence, was in effect acquiescent to the ban on Blacks from the major leagues.

Though Dean was a "moderate" according to one of his biographers, he was still a product of a racially segregated society. In this regard, a simple recognition that ability is colorblind is to be admired. Dean, in his own homespun way, was a racial progressive. Certainly, his honesty did not sit well back home in Arkansas, or in his adopted hometown of St. Louis. "I've pitched thirty-one games against that Satchel Paige," Dizzy declared. "If that guy pitched in the majors, he'd be worth a million dollars."[33]

Kansas City Callin'

J.L. Wilkinson began what would be a lifelong immersion in Black baseball in 1912 with an offensive aggregate he dubbed the "All-Nations team." His team was a conglomerate of Native Americans, Asians, African Americans, whites, and even a woman. The assemblage was not exactly a baseball club; it was something more along the lines of a traveling circus. As they trekked throughout the Mid-west, the All Nations collection would arrive in town, play a ball game, hold a dance, and stage a wrestling match. Some members of the team even played in a band following contests. Though the team began as something of a novelty act, it wasn't long before they developed a reputation for their on-field exploits.

The All-Nations team disbanded in 1918 when World War I and the Selective Service draft tore apart the club's roster. Wilkinson relocated from Des Moines to Kansas City, a town rich in Black baseball tradition. There J.L. formed an all-Black squad, which he dubbed the Monarchs, a name used earlier in the century by another Kansas City based club. Wilkinson's original edition of the Monarchs took the field in 1920 as charter members of the Negro National League though their entry into the NNL was not without reservations.

When Rube Foster was searching for a team to fill out his league lineup, he looked to Kansas City where the original Monarchs had enjoyed great success. Foster tried to put together a club to be owned by his crony Howard Smith, a man with no baseball experience and without the financial where-with-all to back a team. Most importantly, Smith did not hold a lease for the sole acceptable park in Kansas City, the American Association Park. The lease lay with Wilkinson, a man Foster preferred not to deal with if only because of the color of his skin. Out of necessity, however, the league founder and president compromised on the point of all-Black ownership in the NNL and reluctantly allowed Wilkinson to join the league.

Wilkinson's racial heritage proved irrelevant, as he became one of the finest proponents of Black baseball the Negro Leagues would ever know. To his players he was always fair; to the fans of his club, he invariably offered a championship caliber team.

"He was a considerate man, he understood, he knew people," longtime Monarch Newt Allen testified. "Your face could be black as tar; he treated everyone alike. He traveled right along with us."[34]

"Wilkie," as his players called J.L., treated his men as well as any owner in the Negro Leagues. The Monarchs (as well as the All-Nations team) traveled for a time by rail in a custom Pullman car. Later he had a Mack bus made to order so his Monarchs could travel in style. But Wilkinson was more than just a kindly "player's" owner, he was also an innovative administrator.

With baseball suffering from the effects of the Depression, Wilkinson devised a means that would maximize his income and increase the revenue of the Negro Leagues as a whole. J.L.'s radical idea, one that had been attempted only a few times previously, was night baseball.

The Grant Manufacturing Company out of Omaha was hired by Wilkinson to design and construct a portable lighting system for the Monarchs' use. The result consisted of stanchions that could be elevated fifty feet above the field of play. The lights were detachable, which allowed them to be fastened to grandstand roots, and collapsible, for easy transit in the bed of a truck.

Wilkinson's bold initiative was met with great skepticism, but the portable lighting system eventually silenced his critics and proved to be the great salvation of the Negro Leagues. No one benefited more from night baseball, though, than J.L. and the Monarchs. Wilkinson's club would come to rival Greenlee's Crawfords and Posey's Grays as the best that Black baseball had to offer. Before the decade of the thirties was over, Kansas City had passed both outfits to become the elite team in all-Negro ball.

"When they turned that on, it was light as day out," Kansas City pitcher Chet Brewer remembered. "Those lights were beautiful."[35]

Night ball wasn't the only answer to the financial difficulties that came with the Depression. Barnstorming and gimmicks were vital to the economic well being of the league. After his triumph at the 1936 Olympics, Jesse Owens was hired by Wilkinson to perform prior to Monarch games. The great track star would have his speed tested against a variety of challengers. Among the contestants Owens faced were cars, horses, and motorcycles.

Wilkinson was a cunning businessman and knew that a carnival-like atmosphere would draw fans to the ballpark. J.L. also knew and understood baseball, and he never strayed from fielding a competitive club. As the decade drew to a close, Wilkinson began building another championship caliber team. Much to the chagrin of fellow league owners, Wilkinson stole away a number of stars including Cool Papa Bell and Willie Wells. The Monarchs had been dominating the barnstorming trails throughout the Mid-west, but with Wells, Bell, Buck O'Neil, and a reborn Satchel Paige, Kansas City would again rule the Negro Leagues.

A healthy right arm meant that Ol' Satch was again the toast of Black baseball. Everywhere Satchel and the Monarchs traveled, huge crowds appeared and witnessed the best Negro ball had to offer since Greenlee's Crawfords enjoyed their heyday. The attraction of the Monarchs, and of Black baseball in general, began to cross racial boundaries. Though Negro games had always attracted a share of white patronage, as the thirties became the forties the excitement and skill Black clubs brought to the game caught the attention of a wider audience.

Though the Monarchs played the game straight, not all Negro teams relied on talent to draw spectators to the ballpark. A growing faction of Black clubs looked to amuse their crowds with on-field antics that sometimes crossed the line of showmanship and instead demeaned the participants. The Indianapolis Clowns were the worst example of those clubs who perpetuated racial stereotypes that had long dogged Black Americans.

"If you were Black, you were a clown," Piper Davis of the Birmingham Black Barons acknowledged. "Because in the movies, the only time you saw a Black man he was a comedian or butler."[36]

The Indianapolis outfit, though they occasionally fielded a competitive team with promising players, for the most part were little more than a traveling minstrel show. Members of the troupe answered to the ridiculous names of "Monkee," "Tarzan" and "Wahoo." The Zulu Cannibal Giants, while not as well known as the Clowns, were equally devoid of dignity. The Zulus took to the field donning war paint and grass skirts.

A much less offensive form of entertainment employed throughout the Negro Leagues was a game of pantomime called "shadowball." Shadowball enthralled spectators the way the Harlem Globetrotter's captured the attention and thrilled worldwide crowds with the exhibition of their "magic circle" ... sans the ball. The pitcher would toss an imaginary ball plate-ward, where a batter would take a cut at the incoming invisible sphere. Invariably the hitter would make "contact," setting the infield in motion. The players in the field would follow through as if a live ball were in play, scooping and hurling to get the batter (turned base runner) out at first. There were other variations of shadowball, all of which held their audiences' rapt attention. These demonstrations were the manifestation of an unadulterated passion and zeal for the game by men who understood their mission was to entertain, above all else.

Satchel recognized early in his career that showmanship was almost as vital in Black ball as ability. Ads promoting the "Satchel Paige All-Stars" indicated that Satch understood this prerequisite. These placards guaranteed that the star would strike out the first three men he faced ... on nine pitches! The robustly self-confident Paige also was wont to purposely load the bases and proceed to call all of his fielders off the playing surface, leaving just himself and his battery-mate to combat the opponent. Satch would win these self-inflicted conundrums more often than not, but even in failure, the man gave the paying public their money's worth and left them with a desire to return to the "show."

His indecipherable pitches came from a variety of motions; a windmill, a hesitation, and a Model T. These deliveries gave birth to a menagerie of colorful and potent pitches; "Thoughtful Stuff," "Bat Dodger," the "Four Day Rider," the "Hurry Up Ball," the "Wobbly Ball," the "Nothin' Ball," the "Midnight Creeper" and "Long Time."[37] Despite having a litany of pitches in his stable, Satchel's mainstay was his fastball, or "pea" ball, which almost never failed him in a jam.

The much-heralded Paige garnered more attention in the white media than all his Negro League contemporaries combined. *Life*, *Time* and *Saturday Evening Post* all featured profiles of the egocentric right-hander. Those articles cultivated the legend of Paige, increasing the feeling that the integration of baseball was just and past due. Nevertheless, no change regardless how great the need, arrives without resistance.

Satch speculated on the obstacles that would face an integrated world of baseball. "You might as well be honest about it," he wrote. "There would be plenty of problems, not only in the South, where the colored boys wouldn't be able to stay and travel with the teams in spring training, but in the North where they couldn't stay or eat with them in many places. All the nice statements from both sides aren't going to knock out Jim Crow."[38]

All in Due Time

Kenesaw Mountain Landis died on November 24, 1944, and with his passing came the first real hope that baseball's color barrier might be torn down. Landis had long presented himself as the keeper of the game's integrity — the apotheosis of all things honest and true. The Judge maintained this facade throughout his quarter century reign as Baseball's Czar. It is a great irony that no other individual did more to maintain segregation in organized ball than Landis.

When pressure mounted in the late thirties in the Black and radical Left press to desegregate the game, Landis offered, "There is no rule, nor to my knowledge has there ever been, formal or informal, or any understanding, written or unwritten, subterranean or sub-anything against the hiring of Negroes in the major leagues."[39]

While these words may have soothed some, in the wake of World War II the commissioner's words were beginning to sound very hollow — and to fall on disbelieving ears .

Prior to the outbreak of the Second World War, commentary pursuant to the integration of baseball came almost exclusively from the Black press and the Communist paper of record, the *Daily Worker.* The increasingly significant role that Black soldiers were given in America's newly integrated armed forces gave rise to a new open-mindedness that was soon reflected in traditional media outlets. "If Black Americans were good enough to serve and die for their country, they should unquestionably be good enough to play baseball," was an opinion often expressed. During the war years, the major leagues were filled with 4Fs and men too old for the armed service. The player shortage reached such extremes that the St. Louis Browns employed a one-armed outfielder, Pete Gray. Despite the severe lack of manpower, organized ball still couldn't find room for *any* Black player.

A number of Black writers, especially Wendell Smith, Chester Washington, and Joe Bostic, waged a lengthy crusade against baseball's hiring practices. The nation's favorite pastime had long promoted itself as the embodiment of the Democratic process. These journalists dutifully reminded their readers of the hypocrisy enveloped in the notion that "baseball is the great leveler," while a broad segment of the population was not allowed to participate in the profession.

Baseball found it increasingly difficult to preserve the mantle of segregation in the shadow of a war, which at its heart was based on racial superiority. America stood in the forefront of the worldwide struggle for racial equality and tolerance. Her soldiers, both Black and white, gallantly fought an enemy that preached a master race ideology that was systematically eliminating an entire race of people.

In the pages of the *Pittsburgh Courier*, Wendell Smith recognized the discrepancy.

"Baseball is perpetuating the very things thousands of Americans are overseas fighting to end, namely, racial discrimination and segregation."[40] Smith wrote.

This conviction was now being expressed by a few brave souls in the game's management ranks. "Negroes fought alongside whites and shared foxhole dangers, and they should get a fair trial in baseball,"[41] the president of the Montreal Royals, Harold Racin proclaimed in 1946.

Independent thinkers in the game, like Racin, had no opportunity to bring about a change, however, as long as Judge Landis reigned supreme.

Landis's death at the age of seventy-eight fueled speculation concerning his replacement. Baseball's owners waited a respectful interval before naming Albert "Happy" Chandler as the game's second commissioner in April 1945. The choice of Chandler, a senator from Kentucky, dismayed many integration activists who chafed at the thought of a Dixie politician filling the shoes of his racist predecessor.

The new lord of baseball quickly eased such apprehensions. Ric Roberts of the *Pittsburgh Courier* visited Chandler the morning the new commissioner was named to his post. "If a Black boy can make it on Okinawa and Guadalcanal, hell, he can make it in baseball,"[42] Chandler stated to the reporter.

The cynics believed that Chandler was simply pandering to the Black press. One listener, though, was prepared to test the verity of the commissioner's words.

Victory in Europe and Victory in the Pacific were followed in short order by the entrance of a Black man in organized baseball. Just two months after the *Enola Gay* flew her historic mission over Hiroshima, the Brooklyn Dodgers signed Jackie Robinson to a minor league contract. Though the reverberations felt by the concussion of the atom bomb dubbed "Little Boy" were infinitely greater, the news of a Negro joining the ranks of organized baseball shook the game to the core.

Branch Rickey, the Brooklyn Dodgers' general manager, had been preparing to integrate his ball club for several years before signing Robinson. Rickey sent trusted scouts out to find a qualified player for the arduous undertaking. Though none of his scouts touted Robinson as the ideal man, talent-wise, Rickey learned through Wendell Smith that Jackie would be the best suited for integrating the major leagues. Besides being supremely gifted athletically, the college-educated Robinson was more intelligent and articulate than the great majority of his Negro league contemporaries. Regardless of this, Rickey's great aspirations would never have come to fruition without the endorsement of baseball's new commissioner.

With the seven other National League owners banded together in contentious opposition to Rickey's grand plan, only Chandler's words of temperance validated a change of policy and suppressed the rising insurrection among dissenting owners. "I believe Negroes should have a chance like everybody else," Chandler told newsmen. "I believe that this is a free country and everybody should have a chance to play its favorite pastime.... There are reasonable men in baseball, and the ways and means of bringing this about must be worked out."[43]

The broad-minded approach of baseball's new commissioner stood in stark contrast to the beliefs of nearly all of the game's decision makers. His endorsement allowed Rickey to remain true to his principles. Jackie Robinson would play baseball in 1946 with the Montreal Royals of the American Association.

"Somehow I'd always figured it'd be me," Satchel said years after Robinson broke baseball's color barrier. "Those major league owners knew I wouldn't start out with any minor league team like Jackie was.... But signing Jackie like they did still hurt me deep down. I'd been the one who started all that big talk about letting us in the big time. I'd been the one who opened the major league parks to the colored teams. I'd been the one who the white boys wanted to barnstorm against. I'd been the one who everybody said should be in the majors."[44]

Satchel's anger and bitterness were well founded. When the door finally opened, time was not in his favor. Paige had repeatedly displayed his mastery while barnstorming against major league players, yet the glory and riches he assuredly deserved were kept well out of his reach. The anguish of standing by while Robinson received the call was real, but the views he would later espouse sounded to many like sour grapes. Still, even Paige wouldn't deny that the Robinson " experiment" was a success. Following Jackie's fine 1946 campaign with the Montreal club, Rickey elected to bring him to Brooklyn for the '47 season. The Dodger rookie's achievements were extraordinary, especially when examined in light of the adversity he faced as the Majors' first Black participant.

In those early months of the '47 campaign, Robinson distinguished himself as a player, and more importantly, a man. Though the path was rocky and strewn with hurdles, Rickey and Robinson's attainment opened the gateway. In Cleveland, a man long interested in the prospects of bringing Blacks into professional ball was closely watching the happenings in Flatbush.

Bill Veeck, the owner of the American League Cleveland Indians, may have lacked the fortitude it took to sign the first Black to a professional contract, but he didn't shy away from the opportunity to bring an African American to the senior circuit. Like Rickey, who had plucked Robinson from the roster of the Kansas City Monarchs, Veeck dipped into the Negro Leagues and snatched twenty-two year old Larry Doby from the Newark Eagles. Doby, acclaimed by many observers as the best young Negro prospect, appeared in Cleveland's July 5 contest against the Chicago White

Satchel Paige with Bill Veeck (© Bettmann/CORBIS).

Sox without spending a day in the minor leagues. More than half a century of apartheid had finally come to a close.

With the knowledge that the Cleveland owner had previously expressed interest in his talent, Satchel wired Veeck following the signing of Doby: "IS IT TIME TO COME?"

Veeck answered Paige's query with a prompt and cryptic reply. "ALL THINGS IN DUE TIME."[45]

To a man of forty-two, well past his professional prime, who had already tolerated more than two decades of racial intolerance, the irony of Veeck's plea for patience was obvious.

When the call finally did come, however, Satch was ready. With the Indians fighting for a pennant in the heart of 1948, Veeck looked to Paige to help bolster the Cleveland pitching staff. The ancient Paige was brought to Municipal Stadium on July 7 for a surprise tryout for Indian manager Lou Boudreau. Veeck had asked his skipper to venture to the mammoth ball yard to stand in the box "against a young pitcher I thought might help us."[46]

A veteran of the owner's chicanery, Boudreau was no longer surprised by anything the unpredictable Veeck proposed. The Indians' manager kept an open mind and allowed Satchel to display his wares. "I couldn't help but be impressed by his uncanny ability to throw the ball where he wanted," Boudreau later reported. " Satch was in the strike zone four out of every five pitches."[47]

"After we were done," Paige later said, " (Boudreau) told me to go on in the clubhouse. When I walked away, Mr. Lou and Mr. Veeck were up close, real close, jawing away like everything."[48]

A short while later, Veeck approached Paige beneath the stands. "Lou thinks you can help the club," he told Satchel. "Let's go down to the office and sign a contract."[49]

News of the most recent Indian signing did not sit well with all. "Not everybody was happy that I'd gotten into the major leagues," Satchel admitted. "Most were, but there were some who said it was just cheap publicity."[50]

If there was anyone in baseball who would be motivated by the possibility of publicity, it would certainly be the Indians' affable owner. Veeck was known throughout organized ball for his eccentric, attention grabbing gimmicks. These machinations never failed to bring people to the ballpark, which was always Veeck's end goal. Critics believed that the signing of Paige was just another ploy by Veeck to reap bigger gate receipts. The backlash was fierce, and no commentator was more adamant than J. Taylor Spink of *The Sporting News*.

"Veeck has gone too far in his quest for publicity," read Spink's condemnation. "To sign a hurler at Paige's age is to demean the standards of baseball in the big circuits."[51]

The editor of the baseball weekly then added, "Were Satchel white, he would not have drawn a second thought from Veeck." The fact that, had Paige been born of Caucasian parentage, he would have been in the major leagues for decades already, seemingly had not occurred to Spink.

"Maybe Mr. Veeck did want some publicity," Satchel conceded. "But he wanted a pitcher too. There was only one guy around who could fill both orders. That was Ol' Satch."[52]

Ol' Satch's confidence was not misplaced. Dropped into the heat of the pennant race, Paige did not disappoint. Veeck received the publicity he assuredly craved, along with a quality pitcher. The drastic increase at the gate whenever Paige was scheduled to start was just icing on the proverbial cake. (A conservative estimate of 201,829 came to see Paige's final three starts).

The forty-two year old rookie, though lacking the blinding speed he'd possessed in his youth, still kept American League hitters off balance and off kilter. With his wide assortment of pitches and deliveries, Satchel helped propel the Indians to an American League flag. Cleveland finished ahead of Boston's Braves by just one game, and Satchel's contribution of a 6–1 record and 2.48 e. r. a. was certainly a key component of the championship campaign.

Paige's arrival in the big leagues became a circus and Bill Veeck was the ringmaster. Satchel's fine record on the field took a back seat to the playful ruminations in the press that questioned Ol' Satch's date of birth. Veeck, a carnival barker at heart, milked the star power and exoticism that surrounded his ageless pitching wonder.

Reporters, prodded by Veeck, went to great lengths to discover Paige's true age. Satchel insisted, with some leeway for believability, that he was forty-two years young when he made his major league debut. Paige dismissed what became a long running gag, "Man, what you want my birth certificate for?" he asked investigative writers.

"Everybody knows old Satchel was born."[53]

Scores of fans ventured to ball yards throughout the American League to catch a glimpse of the long-limbed legend. Satchel's lively arm fascinated his newfound audience, but it was his unique homespun study of truth that entranced members of the Fourth Estate.

"I'm Satchel," Paige would sometimes offer. "I do as I do."[54]

"My idea of livin' is you gotta keep movin'," the old philosopher explained. "You gotta have lotsa things to do and you gotta do them good. You gotta keep thinkin'. That's why I been able to go so long."[55]

Paige's fruitful '48 season was acknowledged by the same publication that had editorialized against his joining the league. The forty-two (or forty-three or forty-nine...) year-old Satchel was named Rookie of the Year by *The Sporting News.* While he was praised in the mainstream media as a sooth saying folk hero, members of the Black press questioned whether Paige understood the responsibility that came with his new position as a racial pioneer.

"If you were Satchel Paige would you represent your people admirably or would you remain Satchel Paige?"[56] Wendell Smith asked in his *Courier* column.

Smith's was not the sole voice in the Black media to question whether Paige would recognize the duty inherent in his role in baseball's integration process. However, Satchel, unlike Jackie Robinson, wasn't willing to put himself at the forefront of a movement, especially if curtailing his high living was a prerequisite for membership in the vanguard.

Paige continued the bad habits he had perfected in his Negro League days. The major leagues offered a big stage, and Satch was determined to test the waters. Though he was married at the time he was with the Indians, Paige could often be seen with a different woman on his arm each day. For the Indians' official records, Satch claimed to be single. "Well," he told Bill Veeck, "it's like this, I'm not married, but I'm in great demand."[57]

His lechery disturbed many, not excluding Mrs. Paige. Among the offended were commentators in the Black press. These writers believed, with good reason, that for the integration experiment to succeed, Robinson, Doby and Paige must be on their best behavior lest detractors of the movement point to their shortcomings as representative of the entire race. These concerns slowed Paige down not one bit, though his flamboyantly sinful lifestyle drew scarcely veiled barbs in the press.

"It has been reported that Paige hasn't the willpower to give up his playboy antics," Andrew Fay Young wrote in the *Chicago Defender*. "He should not be allowed to jeopardize men like Larry Doby, Jackie Robinson and Roy Campenella, all of whom have acquitted themselves as gentleman on and off the field."[58]

In Paige's defense, however, he never pretended to carry the torch for the Civil Rights movement. Nor did he recognize the social significance of what he and his peers were undertaking. It's fair to say that major league baseball was just another payday for him. Leave the social cares to others, Ol' Satch was gonna do some livin'.

Satchel's marital infidelities weren't the only transgressions that ruffled feathers. His Indian teammates, while it is doubtful that they sat in judgment of his adulterous behavior, deeply resented the special treat-

Satchel Paige and Larry Doby (courtesy NoirTech Research, Inc.).

ment Paige received from Veeck. Paige and his notoriously cavalier attitude toward punctuality irked many of his fellow Indians, including player/manager Lou Boudreau. Satch's struggle with promptness dated back to his Blackball days when he was barnstorming across the land, and the games, more often than not, did not start until the star arrived.

"I ain't braggin'," Satch once said. "But it's true, I got speedin' tickets in most every city in the U.S. Got twelve in Los Angeles in one month. Paid them all, too. The tickets are due to my clock trouble. I always realize I gotta be somewhere after I ain't."[59]

Satch's "clock trouble," as well as his poor training practices, landed him in manager Boudreau's doghouse. As the '48 campaign wound to a close Paige was used less and less. Part of this inactivity could be attributed to Paige's ineffectiveness on the mound: The second and third times around the league, opposing batters were no longer fooled by Satchel's pitching machinations.

Satchel made just one appearance in that fall's World Series, a late game stint in game two of the Indians-Braves match up. Paige's entrance in that contest was the first for a Black pitcher in the Fall Classic. Historic relevance and all, Satchel's effort was little more than a mop-up assignment, as Cleveland was down 11–5 at the time he entered the contest. He retired the two men he faced, while allowing a run to score on a sacrifice fly, and was removed for a pinch hitter at the bottom of the inning.

Paige was disheartened at Boudreau's refusal to utilize him more during the stretch drive, and more importantly the Series. "I felt sick," Satchel later wrote of the experience. "I felt as low as anybody felt.... I just sat in the bullpen hoping and hoping. 'Why?' All I could ask myself, 'Why?" It was the same 'why' I used to ask myself when I couldn't get into the major leagues and there was never an answer."[60]

Self-pity combined with revisionism when Satchel wrote, "If I ever had enough sense to feel bad about baseball, it would be when I put Cleveland in the World Series. I was the greatest pitcher in the American League, but it seems like they pitched everybody else but me in that Series."[61]

The sad truth was, despite his impressive record, Satch was no longer the dominant pitcher he once had been. His early success with the Indians came more from trickery than from the enormous skill he would have brought to the park in his prime. His vaporous fastball was gone; in its place came a variety of "cute stuff" designed to fool batters.

Though white America neglected Paige when he was at the height of his powers, it reveled in the espoused viewpoints Satch put forth for an attentive press corps. A legendary pitcher was transformed into a canonized oracle.

I Do as I Do

Perhaps as much as for his proficiency on the mound, Satchel is remembered for a number of philosophical ramblings accredited to him by the press. The most memorable, "How to Stay Young," was even reprinted in *Bartlett's Familiar Quotations.* These rules of life and how to live it were first published in *Collier's* in 1953.

How to Stay Young

1. If your stomach disputes you, lie down and pacify it with a cool thought.
2. Keep the juices flowing by jangling around gently as you move.
3. Go very lightly on the vices, such as carrying on in society. The social ramble ain't restful.
4. Avoid running at all times.
5. Avoid fried meats which angry up the blood.
6. Don't look back. Something might be gaining on you.[62]

Though "How to Stay Young" was attributed to Paige, it was more likely penned by journalist Richard Donovan. Nevertheless, the charm intrinsic in the prose lay in the fact that Satch *could* have uttered such advice. Paige was fully capable of passing along similar gems of wisdom.

Bases on balls is the curse of the nation.[63]

Ain't no man can avoid being born average, but there ain't no man got to be common.[64]

Such nuggets confirmed Satch's Zen master status, and, as much as anything he would accomplish between the lines, his words established him as a genuine folk hero.

Reporters were smitten with the loquacious Paige, and with good reason. He invariably made good copy, and when Satch didn't come up with an insightful blurb, writers could (and would) easily make one up. Paige never questioned the authenticity of such incidents; they were simply adding to the ever-swelling legend.

It was a most successful marriage. The press ballyhooed Satchel's exploits, fans came out to see the fabled hero perform, and Paige was rewarded with a generous paycheck. Newsmen and magazine profilists added to, and helped maintain, Paige's legendary status. However, these same men also seemed to relish the opportunity to emphasize Satchel's unlettered background. And more than a few reporters used racial stereotypes when describing Satchel's antics.

"Paige, always the showman..." read a 1940 article that appeared in the *Saturday Evening Pos,* "would crank his ape like arms a half dozen times, uncrank them, lean back till he almost lay on the ground, bring that huge left foot up till it almost kicked out a cloud, then would suddenly shoot the ball from somewhere out of this one-man melee."[65] This type of derisive reporting was not reserved for Black athletes. Ethnic slurs and descriptions often found their way into print, as this 1939 *Life* portrait of Joe DiMaggio shows.

"Instead of olive oil or smelly bear grease, he keeps his hair slick with water. He never reeks of garlic and prefers chicken chow-mein to spaghetti."[66]

For Paige "smelly bear grease" would be replaced with "ape like arms," and a glut of Stepin Fetchit imagery crept into many writers expositions. Using Satchel's shuffling gait as a comparison point, reporters likened Paige to the notorious comic film character. Though many in the 1930s Black community took a certain amount of pride in the appearance of a Black actor, *any* Black actor, on the silver screen, Stepin Fetchit's lazy feeble-minded representation of the Black race was nothing but a derogatory caricature written to entertain a culture blinded by racial stereotypes.

White audiences and white writers were comfortable with the facetious and unread Paige; commentators mistook his easygoing manner and enormous ability to diffuse tension with jocularity as complacency. Satchel was not known as a "Race man," nor was he bellicose by any measure. Nevertheless, Paige recognized the injustice that a Black man, even an enormously talented Black man, faced in America.

"I've majored in geography, transportation, and people," Paige once said. "I been a travelin' man."[67] Satchel's treks carried him from a land where the Klan ran free and Strange Fruit swung mournfully from its tree limbs, to towns where he couldn't eat, drink, or relieve himself because of the color of his skin, to a profession that denied equal access and compensation for men of color. Ridiculously, some commentators mistook Satchel's non-militant demeanor as the actions of a "Tom." Even men who claimed to know Paige well perceived Satchel as acquiescent to Jim Crow and all its entrapments.

"Larry (Doby) and Satch represent different eras of American history," Veeck wrote in his autobiography. "Satch never appeared to be interested in fighting battles, changing social patterns or winning acceptance beyond what seems to come to him naturally as a legendary folk hero. Satch wouldn't have been at all upset at not being allowed to stay in our hotel in Tuscon that first year. He would not only have expected to stay across town, he would have preferred it. He doesn't want to go to white restaurants with you and he doesn't want you to go to Negro restaurants with him."[68]

Though considered to be as racially open-minded as men came in mid-twentieth century America, Veeck's psychoanalysis of Paige sells its subject short. Veeck, and others of his ilk, eased their conscience with the belief that men like Paige, who diffused racial anxieties with humor, were satisfied with the status quo.

In his own autobiography Satchel shed light on the genesis of what would be a lifelong tempest kept simmering beneath his exterior. He writes of a child whose juvenile misdeeds were met with corporal punishment at home, of a young man who viewed the inequities he wrestled with through self-indulgent eyes. "I used to think she hit me because she didn't know how I felt," Paige wrote of his mother. "She didn't know how it was when they told me I couldn't swim where the white folks did."[69]

With maturity came the understanding that his mother must have lived with the rejection as well. The source of his desperation, he came to realize, was institutionalized and passed on from one generation to the next.

"She must have been chased away from the white man's swimming places. She must have gotten run off from the white man's stores and stands for just looking hungry at a fish.

"She must have heard those men yelling, 'Get out of here, you no-good nigger.' She must have heard it. I guess she learned how to live with it."[70]

Satch, too, would learn how to "live" with it. He had, however, something his mother and most every other Black in Mobile lacked: an acknowledged commodity. His right arm would ease the frustration, but not dissipate the anger.

"Maybe I got into all those fights because I wasn't very smart and didn't take too good to books," Satchel wrote. "But maybe it was because I found out what it was like to be a Negro in Mobile. Even if you're only seven, eight, or nine, it eats at you when you know you got nothing and can't get a dollar. The blood gets angry. You want to go somewhere, but you're just walking. You don't want to, but you got to walk."[71]

3

In the Shadow of No Man: *Larry Doby*

"I was sixteen and already dreaming of a baseball career," Elston Howard said.

Howard, the first Black to play with the New York Yankees, shared the aspiration of countless African-American youths: the hope of someday playing professional baseball. Their reality, however, allowed them to participate in the Negro Leagues. If they were lucky, perhaps the Kansas City Monarchs would be interested in their services; such was the pinnacle of Negro baseball.

Enter Jackie Robinson, and, in the blink of an eye, the previously unattainable was within reach.

"A friend of mine came into the store and said, 'Ellie, have you heard the news? Branch Rickey has signed one of our boys. His name is Jackie Robinson,'" Howard remembered. "I felt like dancing all over the floor. The path was opening up. Maybe I could become a major league player."[1]

Howard was not alone in his joy. Black America was unified in its celebration of Robinson's momentous chance. The athlete became more than a ballplayer, Robinson signified *opportunity*, opportunity that had previously been denied Black Americans.

At the same time that Branch Rickey signed Robinson to a professional contract, Larry Doby was in his final months of Navy service, stationed on the South Pacific island of Ulitihi, some 900 miles from the beaches of Iwo Jima. Doby whiled away the time following the Japanese surrender, in playing ball with fellow servicemen, among them major league players Mickey Vernon and Billy Goodman.

The news of Robinson's signing reached the island quickly.

On Ulitihi, Larry was sitting by a radio when he heard the news.

Doby's plans of becoming a teacher, or perhaps a coach, back home in New Jersey were replaced by the possibility of a career in major league baseball.

Major league baseball was no longer an all-white domain. Vernon, cognizant of Doby's exceptional abilities, turned to his comrade in arms. " You've got a chance now, Larry," Vernon told Doby. "The next one could be you."[2]

Larry Doby's youth was spent on the playgrounds and ball fields of Paterson, New Jersey. In addition to starring at Eastside High School, Larry played recreation league basketball where he encountered a man named Wendell Williams, who shared with the youth his knowledge of Black self-awareness.

Williams educated the young men about great Black leaders like Frederick Douglass, W.E.B. Du Bois, and Paul Robeson. As a teenager, Larry didn't fully appreciate the message that Williams was attempting to impress upon the youngsters "It may have been a blessing that we didn't understand Wendell Williams about a quota system," Larry said years later. "If we had a chip on our shoulders, the white kids wouldn't understand us because they themselves would not treat us in a way that would cause us to behave in the militant way Williams wanted."

"I had never known segregation growing up," Doby claimed. "I lived in South Carolina until I was twelve, and most of the kids weren't ever concerned with race. Then, we moved to Paterson and I lived in a mixed neighborhood. Nobody ever called me a name, I never had a problem."[3]

Even in his role as a civil rights pioneer Larry never played the militant. The lessons taught by Williams, however, did leave a mark on young Doby. "Economics is at the basis of our problems as Negroes," Doby said following his retirement as an active player. "Education and job opportunities go hand in hand.... We Negroes try to succeed through necessity; we should try to succeed as our natural right. If we fail, pressure builds up, we become tight, can't relieve the pressure and sometimes explode."[4]

Doby was fortunate; he had sports to alleviate some of the burden imposed upon him as a Black American. At Eastside High School, Doby excelled as one of New Jersey's finest athletes. By the time he graduated, Larry had earned eleven varsity letters in track, baseball, basketball, and football. In baseball, Doby made the all New Jersey team as a first baseman in his junior year. The next season he was named an all-state second baseman.

Doby graduated from Eastside on June 24, 1942. Less than a month earlier, performing under the alias of "Larry Walker," Doby made his professional debut at Yankee Stadium. Playing for the Newark Eagles, Larry went one-for-four with a single in his initial contest.

Abe and Effa Manley, the owners of the Eagles, gave Larry $300 to play for Newark until the start of school that fall. Despite his youth, Larry's arrival sparked a renewal on the Newark club.

"Signing of Larry Walker Rejuvenates Newark Eagles,"[5] read the headline in the *New Jersey Afro-American.* Larry's initial professional season was a resounding success. Though some box scores are missing from his rookie year, information gathered from salvaged box scores tell of a .391 batting average for the 18-year-old "Walker."

Following the season, Larry attended Long Island University, where he played on the school's basketball team. Just one month after the conclusion of the basketball season Doby received his draft notice. Subsequent to his graduation from Great Lakes Naval Training Station, Larry was assigned to Ulitihi a tiny island in the South Pacific. The men stationed on the island supplied fuel for aircraft and ships in support of General Douglas MacArthur's Pacific fleet. There on Ulitihi, Doby stayed until January 1946 when he received his honorable discharge from the Navy.

Years later Larry would claim that he never confronted segregation until he entered the Navy. " For the first time I was conscious of discrimination and segregation as never before. I thought: 'this is a crying shame when I'm here to protect my country.' But I couldn't do anything about it. I was under Navy rules and regulations and had to abide by them or face the consequences."[6]

Though Doby may not have been "consciously" aware of his surrounding environment and politics during his adolescent life, institutionalized and cryptic segregation surrounded his being.

Paterson's local theatre, the Majestic, confined Black patrons to its third balcony, which was known as "Nigger Heaven." Larry was also excluded from several athletic opportunities because of the pigmentation of his skin. His high school basketball coach, Henry Rumona, held a summer camp every year, yet Doby was never invited to participate. Doby also failed to acknowledge the obvious: he played for the all-Black Newark Eagles prior to his entry in the Navy.

Clearly the various slights and degrading circumstances that colored his youth paled in comparison with the disgraceful politics encountered once he entered the Navy. This discovery was exacerbated when Doby placed it into context: he was contributing to an effort that would preserve democracy, yet as an American Black he was not considered the equal of white servicemen by his own government.

Following the war, Doby returned home in time to earn $500 a month with the San Juan club in the Puerto Rican winter leagues. Larry discovered that his time spent in the service to his nation had not eroded his baseball skills.

Rejoining Newark that spring, Larry batted .348 for the '46 season. The Eagles, as the finest club in the Negro National League, were pitted against the Kansas City Monarchs in the Negro World Series. Newark won the championship in seven games, while Larry batted .272 in the series.

Jackie Robinson spent the 1946 season with the Brooklyn Dodgers' affiliate in Montreal. Robinson's year with the International League Royals was a complete triumph on the playing field. Branch Rickey's painstaking investigation and scouting of Robinson had not been in vain. In Robinson Rickey had found a man equal to the hour.

Bill Veeck of the Cleveland Indians recognized the progress of Rickey's grand experiment and decided to act.

"Robinson has proved to be a real big leaguer, so I wanted to get the best of the Negro boys while the grabbing was good," Veeck explained. "Why wait? Within ten years Negro players will be in regular service with all big league teams, for there are many colored players with sufficient capabilities to make the majors."[7]

"When I came to Cleveland," Veeck explained, "I was almost sure I was going to sign a Negro player. We were drawing better than Brooklyn, that wasn't a factor. I simply couldn't find, at those prices, a ball player with similar talent.

"I had informed the scouts that I wasn't necessarily looking for the best player in the Negro Leagues, but the player with the best long term potential."[8]

Veeck believed that Cleveland would be receptive to a Black player. Paul Brown had integrated the city's professional football team, the Cleveland Browns, the previous fall with no incident. With this in mind, Veeck sent his scouts out to locate a player who would meet his qualifications. In preparation Veeck also hired an African American, Louis Jones, as a public relations man, who would prepare Cleveland's Black community for the integration of the Indians. Jones' position served a dual purpose; he would also be a companion for Larry on the road.

One name consistently came up as Veeck's scouts surveyed the Negro Leagues: Larry Doby. Indian scout Bill Killifer spent the better part of two months studying Doby before returning a flattering report on the Newark second baseman.

Veeck heeded Killifer's knowledgeable advice, and decided to sign Doby to a Cleveland contract. The Indians owner sent Jones to prepare Doby for the monumental task that lay ahead. Jones informed Doby that he would be with the Cleveland organization within two or three weeks. Larry, however, believed Jones was joking and thought little of the exchange until his contract was actually purchased by Cleveland.

Thanks to his fine play, the twenty-two year old Larry Doby was a fan favorite in Newark, and with good reason. In 1946, Larry batted .341 for the Eagles while leading them to the Eastern Negro League pennant, and caught the final out of game seven as the Monarchs took the Negro World Series.

Larry's performance in 1946 moved him to the forefront of young Black stars. Still, despite Jackie Robinson's successful season in Montreal, Larry believed he would have to wait some time for his shot at the majors because of his youth.

On July 1, Veeck phoned Effa Manley, the Eagles owner, and informed her of his desire to bring Doby to the major leagues.

"What do you plan to give me?" Manley asked.

"$10,000," Veeck replied.

"You know very well that if he were a white boy you'd give me $100,000," Manley brazenly said.

"Well," Veeck countered, "I'll send $5,000 more if he sticks."[9]

Manley was in no position to argue. Had she refused Veeck's offer, Negro League fans would never have forgiven her, and she would have been crucified by the Black press for denying Doby the opportunity. For that matter, Veeck, as Branch Rickey had done in the case of Jackie Robinson, could have filched Doby away without paying a cent to the Manleys.

In his own mind Rickey easily justified his deplorable actions. The Negro Leagues were, he said, " a front for a monopolistic game controlled by booking agents in Chicago, Philadelphia, and New York.

"They [the Negro Leagues] are the poorest excuse for the word league and by comparison with organized baseball, which they understandably try to copy. They are not leagues at all. I fail to find a single player under contract, and learned that players of all teams become free agents at the end of the season."[10]

"Who was he to criticize?" Effa Manley asked. "Who was he to discuss illegal activities? He took players from the Negro Leagues and didn't ever pay for them. How legal is that? I'd call it a racket."[11]

Manley wasn't the first, nor would she be the last, to imply that Rickey harbored some hypocritical tendencies. The "Mahatma," as some reporters referred to Rickey, was a supreme egotist. He relished the title bestowed upon him as Baseball's "Great Emancipator" and he never failed to regale listeners with the tale of his role in the game's integration. His motivations behind the Robinson signing were divinely inspired, Rickey would imply. His critics, however, were apt to judge Rickey's actions as financially motivated. Robinson was simply a dollar sign to Rickey, these commentators believed.

Despite their comparable positions in the destruction of segregation of the national pastime, Veeck and Rickey could not have had more disparate personalities. A man of letters, Rickey spoke in polysyllabic dissertations, ramblings that were as likely to invoke Scripture or Abraham Lincoln, as Casey Stengel or Rogers Hornsby.

Branch Rickey thought well of himself, and liked to believe that he, "the Mahatma," was above the fray. In stark contrast, Veeck portrayed himself as "a man of the people." The Indians' owner curried the favor of Cleveland fans, often creating promotions and giveaways to keep his customers happy. Rickey disdained these practices, and firmly held the belief that the game was on a higher plane, not some carnival sideshow.

Though Veeck sincerely believed that Blacks deserved and earned a place in the game, he did not cloak his actions in the guise of morality. Veeck brought Doby on board because it was the right thing to do, but more importantly, to win games. Undoubtedly Veeck possessed a healthy ego himself, however unlike Rickey he did not portray himself as a hero to the press.

While Rickey assiduously planned every aspect of Robinson's introduction to professional baseball, Veeck simply signed a qualified player. "I'm not going to sign a Negro player and send him to a farm club," he said. " I'm going to get one I think can play with Cleveland. One afternoon when the team trots on the field, a Negro player will be out there with them."[12]

On July 3, Cleveland's Black newspaper, the *Call and Post*, reported that the Indians had signed Doby. The paper had scooped Veeck, who hoped to keep the signing quiet for another week. Veeck had planned on debuting Larry on July 10 when the Indians were scheduled to play at home, but the *Call and Post* sped up his timetable.

"Once the story was in the papers," Veeck told Doby's biographer Joseph Thomas Moore, "I didn't want a period of speculation. I figured this would have made Larry more distraught, put increased pressure on him."[13]

After learning of the story in the *Call and Post,* Veeck hurriedly contacted his manager, Lou Boudreau, and told him of his intentions. Following the meeting in which, according to Veeck, Boudreau reacted "extremely well," the manager met with the press in the team's Chicago hotel.

"Creed, race, and color are not factors in baseball success, whether it be in the major or minor leagues," Boudreau told the gaggle of gathered scribes. "Ability and character are the only factors.

"Doby will be given every chance, as will any other deserving recruit, to prove that he has the ability to make good with us."[14] The Indians' public relations department prepared the statement, and Boudreau placed his signature beneath the proclamation without hesitation.

Doby's final appearance with Newark came on July 4 during the first game of a doubleheader. At the time, Larry was leading the NNL in batting with an average of .415, and in home runs with 14. Befitting the fine season he was having up to that point, Larry ended his Negro League career with a home run in his final at bat.

Following the first half of the scheduled twin bill, Louis Jones informed Doby that he would be in Chicago the next day as a member of the Cleveland Indians. "Do you want to fly, or go by train?" Jones asked the dumbfounded player.

"If it's all the same to you, I'd rather go by train," Larry replied. "You see, this is a big opportunity for me and I don't want to miss it."[15]

Before the second game a spur-of-the-moment salute to Doby was held at home plate. During the brief ceremony Larry was given a shaving kit and a traveling bag by his teammates. He humbly accepted the modest gift, thanked the crowd and retreated to the locker room, where he prepared for his journey to the Windy City and big league baseball.

In Chicago, Jones and Doby hailed a cab and immediately headed to the Congress Hotel. At the hotel, they would pick up Veeck and proceed to Comiskey Park, home to Chicago's White Sox. There, in the back seat of the taxi, Doby met Bill Veeck for the first time.

"Lawrence you are going to be part of history," Veeck told Doby. " There are thousands of Black youngsters awaiting your footsteps."[16]

The Indians' owner advised Larry of several ground rules unique to his role as the league's first Black: "No arguing with umpires. Don't even turn around at a bad call at the plate, and no dissertations with opposing players; either of those might start a race riot. Remember to act in a way that you know people are watching you."[17]

Veeck hoped to soothe the obviously overwhelmed and intimidated Doby, who had less than twenty-four hours to prepare for the daunting task that lay ahead. "Just remember, they play with a little white ball up here just like they did in your league," he advised. "Remember, we're in this together."[18]

Arriving at Comiskey Park, Doby and Veeck met with the media. Simultaneous with the press conference, Boudreau addressed his club. "He will be a part of our team," the manager said. "He'll be wearing the same uniform as we are, so we'll fight for him as well as you'd fight for me or anyone else. Just as you fellows have to earn your job, he's going to be treated the same way."[19]

Larry Doby of the Cleveland Indians (© Bettman/ CORBIS).

Following the press conference, Larry made his way to the Cleveland clubhouse where he met his new teammates. Boudreau stepped forward and greeted his newest player.

"Hi ya Larry, I am very happy to meet you."

"Thank you Mr. Boudreau," Doby quietly said. "I am very glad to meet you."

The manager then took Larry around the room and personally introduced him to the individual players.

"Joe Gordon, Larry Doby,"[20] Boudreau said to his second basemen, who took Larry's outstretched hand and firmly clasped it.

The duo moved on to the next locker, the introductions were repeated, but Larry's offered hand was ignored. This show of disdain recurred several times throughout the clubhouse.

"I don't know why people say I was accepted," Larry later said. "People didn't write it. They wrote about Jackie Robinson, but the same thing happened in the American League. This wasn't supposed to happen. This is America ... mine was worse than Jackie Robinson. The American League was the top of baseball, while the National League was like a bush league, really.

"One of the things other teams would yell at me was, 'You're not supposed to be in this league. You're supposed to be in that bush league with that other nigger."[21]

Veeck had learned of the hostile reaction felt in some segments of the

Indians' clubhouse, and addressed this concern the day before Doby's arrival.

"I understand that some of you players have said that, 'if a nigger joins the club you're leaving. Well, you can leave right now because this guy is going to be a bigger star than any guy in this room.[22]

"Some of my teammates said they wouldn't play if I did," Larry reported. "What happened? Mr. Veeck eventually got rid of them. But I don't reveal names. I just hope their consciences are clear. Sure, I've forgiven them. Some people made it tough for me, but I hold no grudges. I harbor no ill will."[23]

Joe Gordon was one of the few men who, in his own modest manner, made Doby feel welcome. After the team left the clubhouse and took the field, Gordon called out to Doby to grab a glove. The two men warmed up together under the gaze of thousands in the stands, and more than a few hard glares from players on the field.

Larry recognized, and appreciated the gesture made by Gordon and the handful of men who attempted to make him feel at ease. "It wasn't the easiest thing for them to do," Larry acknowledged. "If they showed too much generosity towards [me], they could have lost social stature."[24]

Eleven weeks after Jackie Robinson first appeared in a Brooklyn Dodgers uniform, Larry Doby integrated the American League.

In the seventh inning of Cleveland's July 5 contest against Chicago, Boudreau inserted Doby into the game as a pinch hitter. ("I was so scared, I didn't even know how many men were out,"[25] Doby remembered) Facing right-hander Earl Harrist, Larry struck out. As he returned to the Cleveland bench, Larry's manager patted him on the back, "Well now you know what it is all about," Boudreau said sympathetically. "You are now a big leaguer."[26]

Cleveland Jackson dramatically described Doby's first appearance in the pages of the *Call and Post.* "For Larry Doby it took but a few short minutes to walk up to the plate," Jackson penned. "But for 13 million American Negroes that simple action was the successful climax of a long up-hill fight whose annals are like the saga of the race."[27]

The following afternoon, Larry started his first, and only, game of the season when Boudreau penciled his name in the lineup as the Indians' first baseman. Because his natural position was second base, Doby needed a first baseman's glove. When teammate Eddie Robinson was asked by Boudreau to loan his glove to Doby, he refused. Robinson only relented when Spud Goldstein, the team's traveling secretary, asked if he would lend the glove to *him.* Robinson acquiesced; Goldstein then proceeded to give the mitt to Larry.

The Robinson incident underscored to Larry that his journey as a baseball pioneer would not be smooth sailing. Upon leaving Comiskey Park after his first game Doby, accompanied by Louis Jones, went, not to the Del Prado Hotel with his teammates, but to the all-Black Du Sable Hotel. This practice would be repeated in every American League city other than New York and Boston.

"I had no roommates on trips," Doby explained. "On trains no one invited me to play cards or talk over games. The worst thing was not having anyone to communicate with, talk over the game with after its over and start me thinking about the next game ... it was very lonely."[28]

An occurrence in St. Louis threatened to hinder, if not completely stifle, the progress of Doby's integration. Throughout a game against the Browns a fan showered Doby with vile racial slurs. Under the nonstop barrage of epithets, Larry lost his composure, grabbed a bat, and attempted to climb into the grandstand to silence the offending party. If not for the intervention of coach Bill McKechnie, Doby's career might have ended with the angry outburst.

In a separate contest an infielder spat on Larry as he slid into second base.

"I just thank God there was an umpire there named Bill Summers, who kind of walked between us when I was ready to move on this fella,"[29] Doby said.

"Larry was not a man to shake off those earlier slights and insults that easily," Bill Veeck said. "He was always very sensitive. If he wanted to dispute an umpire's call, he would back off and point to the back of his hand, as if to say, 'You called that on me because I'm colored.'"[30]

Boudreau scarcely used Larry for the remainder of the '47 season. When the year came to a close, Doby had appeared in just twenty-nine games, almost exclusively as a pinch-hitter. Larry came to bat thirty-two times, collecting only five hits and one walk.

Boudreau recognized that Doby's performance was being adversely affected by the immense strain that accompanied Larry's unique position. To protect what he believed to be a promising future, Boudreau removed Doby from his plans for the remainder of the '47 season, opting instead to ready Larry for his sophomore campaign.

The first step in preparing for the '48 season was finding Larry a new position. "Joe Gordon is the second baseman and he's going to be here awhile," McKechnie told Larry, "When you go home this winter get a book and learn how to play the outfield."[31]

Doby heeded his coach's advice. When Larry returned home to Paterson, New Jersey he visited the local library and borrowed *How to Play the*

Outfield, a book written by New York Yankee star Tommy Henrich. Larry's home schooling was put to use when the Indians commenced spring training on March 1 in Tucson, Arizona.

Before taking his newly learned skills to the field, however, Larry was confronted with another row of indignities. Shortly after arriving in Tucson, Doby learned that he would be forced to live separately from his teammates. The manager of the Indians spring training home, the Santa Rita hotel, claimed that Doby's presence would "hurt business." Spud Goldstein was forced to scramble and find Larry accommodations with a local Black family.

Though Veeck knew of the Jim Crow atmosphere Jackie Robinson endured during his training camp in Florida, he had no idea that Doby would suffer the same humiliation in Arizona. If Veeck faltered in his otherwise noble decision to integrate the senior circuit, it was in his failure to anticipate a great number of variables that would confront Larry.

"We weren't able to talk the management into allowing Larry to stay with us in his first year, although we did make it clear — and they agreed — that in the future they would take all of our players, regardless of race, creed or previous condition of servitude,"[32] Veeck wrote in his memoirs. "It was easy enough for me to tell Larry that these things took time. It was true enough to say that we had, after all, broken through one color barrier even if he was going to have to wait a year. It was easy for me, because it was he who was being told to be patient and wait."[33]

Perhaps hoping to disguise his poor planning, Veeck "misremembered" the facts of the matter. The Indians continued to stay at the Santa Rita until 1954, while Doby and all his future Black teammates stayed with Black families during spring training.

Little attention was given to the segregated conditions Larry suffered. The Cleveland media barely mentioned the circumstances, and Doby's teammates hardly noticed that he disappeared following games. Regardless of the dehumanizing circumstances, Larry enjoyed a productive and eye-opening camp.

Under the tutelage of former Cleveland great Tris Speaker, Doby flourished at his new outfield position. Speaker tirelessly hit Larry fly balls and taught his apprentice the finer aspects of playing the field. Gordon Cobbledick of the *Cleveland Plain Dealer* noticed the marked change in Doby.

"The biggest difference between the Doby of 1948 and the Doby of a few months ago is found in the complete absence of the tension that made it impossible for him to display his talents to good advantage last season," Cobbledick wrote.

"With the tension gone, he has earned new respect from the other Indians by showing what he never was able to show before — namely, that he is a richly gifted young athlete with a better than even chance to become a top flight big league star."[34]

Larry enjoyed a fine spring. His .358 batting average was second only to Boudreau's. The highlight of the exhibition season was Doby's monstrous 500-foot home run in front of a hostile Texarkana crowd. Larry's prodigious blast not only quieted the vicious onslaught of verbal abuse, but also fostered acceptance among fellow Indians.

Thanks to his performance during the spring campaign, Larry proved his potential value to the team, and convinced his critics that he rightfully belonged on the club.

On Tuesday, April 20, the Indians opened the 1948 season, with Larry Doby starting in right field. More than 2.6 million fans passed through the turnstiles at Cleveland's Municipal Stadium and witnessed the most exciting campaign in franchise history. The Indians finished the '48 season tied with the Boston Red Sox with a record of 96-58. The first playoff in the game's history was held on October 5 to determine who would face the Boston Braves in the fall classic.

Perhaps more than any other member of the Indians, Doby propelled the club toward the pennant. Throughout the final twenty games of the season, Larry's performance was extraordinary. During that three-week span, Doby batted .396 with three home runs and ten runs batted in. In addition, Larry's two hits in Cleveland's 6-3 victory over the Red Sox hiked his season average to .301 and pushed Cleveland into the Series. On the field, like Jackie Robinson in his first season, Larry defined himself as a productive major league player and not just an experiment in racial progress.

In the World Series, the Indians jumped out to a two games to one lead against the Braves. 81,000 fans viewed Game Four of the Series. The lucky fans in Cleveland Stadium and witnessed the hometown team climb to within one game of their first world championship since 1920. The advantage was made possible by Doby's fourth inning smash off Johnny Sain, which resulted in a 2-1 victory for Cleveland.

Following the contest, Steve Gromek, the winning pitcher, grabbed Doby in a joyous embrace. Without reserve, the pitcher wrapped his burly arms around Larry's neck as each man exploded in an ear-to-ear grin. This honest and heartfelt display was captured by a photographer and would be seen in the sports pages all across the country the next morning.

The photo of Gromek and Doby, the warm embrace between a Black man and a white man, stunned many of its viewers, so rare was such a

Teammates: Steve Gromek and Larry Doby (AP/ Wide World photographs).

sight in 1948. The meaning of the picture, symbolically and literally, was not lost on Doby.

"The picture was more rewarding and happy for me than actually hitting the home run," Larry told Joseph Thomas Moore. "It was such a scuffle for me, after being involved in all that segregation, going through all I had to go through, until that picture. The picture finally showed a moment of a man showing his feelings for me."[35]

Doby believed that more could be read into the photograph than just a quick snapshot of a festive clubhouse celebration. "The picture is not just about me," he said. "It shows what feelings should be, regardless of differences among people. And it shows what feelings should be in all life, not just sports. I think enlightenment can come from such a picture."[36]

Subsequent to viewing the image, Majorie MacKenzie of the *Pittsburgh Courier* penned, "The chief message of the Doby-Gromek picture is acceptance."[37]

This one simple measure of unabashed affection held vast meaning for Larry Doby. Still a simple black and white photograph would not end racial difficulties in the major leagues or the country at large. Discrimination and segregation would continue to plague players of color. Epithets would continue to pour out of opposing dugouts and rain down from the stands. Despite MacKenzie's interpretation of the Doby-Gromek photo, however insightful, general acceptance remained a distant vision.

The Indians finished off the Braves in six games to claim the 1948 World

Paterson, New Jersey, welcomes home a native son Larry Doby and his wife, Helyn (©Bettmann/CORBIS).

Championship. Larry's heroics in the 1948 campaign were celebrated in his hometown of Paterson. Following the World Series, Doby was greeted with a banner, ("Welcome Home Larry Doby Paterson Is Proud Of You") and a parade held in his honor. Shortly after the modest ceremony, however, Larry understood just how welcome he and his wife Helyn were, when the couple tried to buy a house with his share of the winnings from the Series.

A petition was circulated in an effort to keep the Dobys from infiltrating an all-white neighborhood. Eventually Larry bought a home, but only after the mayor of Paterson intervened on his behalf.

"In 1948 I got the opportunity to play everyday and show what I could do," Doby said. "When you talk about those early days, you're talking about the times and what it was like for men of color. Things were not always right but we felt we had to go along with it. I concentrated on playing baseball and that kept my mind off other things."[38]

With his contribution to the Series victory, Doby established himself as one of the game's premier players. Any doubt of Larry's position amongst his peers was put to rest with his productive 1950 effort. For that year, Larry batted .326, belted 25 home runs, drove in 102 runs, and scored 110 times.

After a slightly down year in 1951 Doby responded with three straight stellar seasons. Again in 1954, the Indians represented their league in the fall classic. On this occasion however, Cleveland failed to taste the champagne. The Indians lost the '54 Series in four straight to the New York Giants.

Larry played one more season in Cleveland, and then on October 25, 1955 he found himself traded to the Chicago White Sox. In exchange for Larry, the Indians received outfielder Jim Busby and infielder Chico Carrasquel. In the pages of the *Cleveland Press* columnist Franklin Lewis gave Larry a rancorous sendoff.

"Larry Doby whose opportunities for immortality in baseball ended where his complexes began — at the neckline — was in a greener pasture today," Lewis wrote. "The Indians got the worst of the bargain, though this does not mean that I consider the departure of Doby a calamity to baseball in Cleveland. He has been a controversial athlete. Highly gifted, he was frequently morose, sullen and upon occasion, downright surly to his teammates.... He thought of himself, at the beginning, as the symbol of the Negro in his league. In later years he overcame this singular complex to a degree, because he beat back his temper and quit throwing bats and giving other visible evidences in his profession."[39]

Like many of his contemporaries, Lewis refused to accept that Doby and Robinson *were* symbols to their people. Perhaps the "sullen" and "morose" behavior described by Lewis was a product of the intolerance he may have faced in this role

Doby dismissed Lewis's assertions out of hand. "I was looked on as a Black man, not as a human being," he said, "a gentleman who carried himself in a way that people would respect. I did feel a responsibility to the Black players who came after me, but that was a responsibility, basically, to people, not just to Black people."[40]

Larry described the deportment that Lewis disapproved of as "a responsibility that called for all the dignity and diplomacy that had to be used, because I was involved in a historical and pioneering life. I could probably have been like an [Luke] Easter or a [Satchel] Paige, but that wasn't my role. I think that I have gained some dignity and respect from those who have looked at me differently from what they were taught to expect from a Black man, or different from what they were used to."[41]

Larry struck a blow for racial equality in sports in the most unintentional acts. With what *Ebony* magazine dubbed a "symbolic left hook,"[42] Doby became the first Black player to engage in a fight on the playing field.

On June 13, 1957, Art Ditmar of the Yankees sent Larry sprawling with a brush-back pitch. Throughout his career Larry, like most pioneering Blacks in professional ball, had found himself a target at the plate. "People forget that in those years most of the Black players still played in the National League," Doby reminded listeners. "In American League cities, there were a lot of bench jockeys who never let up on me and said things. I shrugged it off because I had been told I couldn't fight back.

"It never came to fisticuffs. I couldn't let that happen. But that's what the bench-jockeys wanted — an incident. They wanted an excuse to get me and Jackie banned from the majors. We both knew if it happened it might take years before more Blacks could be signed."[43]

Ditmar's vicious delivery, however, triggered something in Larry.

Doby instantly rose to his feet, and in a flash was at the mound dispensing a left hook to Ditmar's jaw. Not surprisingly, Doby's violent outburst triggered a lengthy bench-clearing brawl.

"There is no intent here to condone what Doby did," Shirley Povich wrote in *The Washington Post*, "merely to point out that the consequences fell far short of Civil War, or secession, or a violent sense of outrage except among Ditmar's Yankee teammates who dashed to his assistance, but in no more anger than if his attacker had been a white player....

"Now this was no white pitcher dusting off a Negro batter simply because of the difference in pigmentation. But the Doby-Ditmar episode had special significance because for the first time a Negro player was daring to get as assertive as the white man whose special province Organized Ball had been for nearly a hundred years."[44]

Unfortunately, the first interracial fight on a major league field was one of the last times Larry made headlines as a player. In the midst of diminishing productivity Larry found himself playing with four different clubs in the final season of his career.

Doby retired at the close of the 1959 season with very respectable career numbers, hit 253 home runs during the course of his career while driving in 969 runs.

"Knowing what I know now," Larry said. "I do look back on my playing career with some anger. But that's because I now understand the impact of all I and the other Black players went through. I'm fortunate that God let me concentrate on baseball and not on the other things."[45]

The Walls Come Tumbling Down

Jackie Robinson is reported to possess baseball abilities which, were he white, would make him eligible for a trial with, let us say, the Brooklyn Dodger Class C farm at Newport News, if he were six years younger.

The Sporting News, November 1, 1945

Jackie Robinson (©Bettmann/CORBIS).

The same weekly paper that criticized Robinson's signing self-righteously declared baseball's "race problem" over with the arrival of Larry Doby in Cleveland.

"Just so long as there was a Negro ballplayer in the National League—Jackie Robinson, with Brooklyn and none in the American League, there was a Negro question in the majors," read an editorial in Baseball's Bible, *The Sporting News*. "Now that the Cleveland club has placed Larry Doby, a first baseman acquired from the Newark team of the Negro National League, on its roster, the race matter no longer is an official perplexity. It no longer exists insofar as Organized Baseball administration is concerned."[46]

The paper's stance following baseball's integration came as no surprise, especially in light of the fact that the "no ban on Blacks" line was trumpeted by the conservative weekly prior to Robinson's signing. Half a century of Jim Crowism in the national pastime had been wiped out by the emergence of two Black participants. This evaluation, that if no problem exists, then there is no problem to fix, was sorely misguided. Just two of the major leagues sixteen teams employed Blacks at the time the editorial was published, though the St. Louis Browns would join the ranks of the edified on July 17, 1947 when they signed Hank Thompson and Willard Brown to major league contracts. The Browns, according to *The Sporting News*, signed the duo purely for financial gain: Had the club been interested in improving its play on the field, they most certainly would have signed better qualified white players.

By the spring of 1951, the Cleveland organization remained the most open-minded in the American League. The Indians went through spring training with four Blacks on their roster. Joining Doby and Luke Easter were "Suitcase" Harry Simpson and Minnie Minoso. Unfortunately, not all four would open the season in Cleveland. Just prior to opening day, as part of a three-team deal, Minoso was traded to the Chicago White Sox for pitcher Lou Brisse. Minoso, despite possessing great promise, was dealt purely to limit the number of Blacks on the squad.

"We heard that Greenberg had to make a choice," Doby said, referring to Indians general manager Hank Greenberg. "He kept Simpson because he was a long ball hitter, which fit into Greenberg's pattern of thinking. Until then, the Black players never talked about the quota. We just thought how strong we were going to be with the four of us, and how happy we were going to be with four of us together."[47]

However slowly, tolerance of Blacks in the majors increased throughout the league. Still there were limits to this acceptance. As the decade of the fifties began, more than half of the major leagues teams remained lily-white. Four Blacks on one club was widely considered to be excessive, regardless of the talent level of the players in question.

Minoso exemplified this obtuse policy. In his first season with the White Sox Minoso led the American League in triples and stolen bases while batting .324. These transactions of convenience were largely ignored in the mainstream press. The failure of the media to take note of these matters could be explained perhaps by the fact that only two clubs were in danger of having too many Blacks, Brooklyn and Cleveland.

Just a couple of years after the Minoso transaction, the Indians increased the number of minorities on the team from three to five. "We have five of *them,*" was a common complaint in Cleveland, "and that's at least three too many." The hierarchy of the game held a belief that "too many Blacks" on one club was not "good business."

In both Brooklyn and Cleveland, the additions of Black players increased attendance and helped produce immediate pennants. Still, other league owners were agonizingly slow to follow suit. While a handful of teams added Blacks to their rosters, some franchises were steadfast in their refusal to integrate.

"It's reasonably certain that there are some clubs in both major leagues which prefer to operate with all-white casts,"[48] a contemporary commentator opined. By 1950, only six Blacks were in the majors, and *six* years after Robinson joined the Dodgers, only six clubs had integrated.

The last franchise to sign a Black to an organizational contract, the Detroit Tigers, integrated only after the club's owner passed away. That the team waited until Walter O. Briggs had died was not coincidental. "The saying around the clubhouse was 'no jigs with Briggs…,'" Edgar

Hayes, a sports editor of the *Detroit Times* remembered. "[Briggs] was dead set against having any Blacks play for him.... It was well known that any scout who signed a colored player would be fired."[49]

Reporter Michael Betzhold wrote in *Queen of Diamonds, The Tiger Stadium Story,* "In Detroit's large and growing Black community in the 1950's, the Briggs name was synonymous with racism."[50]

Briggs wasn't alone in his racist beliefs. For every Bill Veeck, there were five Connie Macks or Robert Carpenters, men who vowed that their clubs would remain virginal white regardless of the progress being made throughout the remainder of the league.

Among the owners, Mack was the one of the fiercest opponents of integration. The legendary owner/manager of the Philadelphia A's had the opportunity to sign both Doby and Minoso for $5,000 apiece, and later Henry Aaron for $3,500. Instead Mack patiently waited for a "qualified" player, and refused to "exploit just anyone in order to draw fans."[51]

Perhaps more than any other club, the Boston Red Sox vacillated before adding a Black to their team. Sam Lacy noted in the pages of the *Baltimore Afro-American* that "the Red Sox will never have a regular colored player as long as Yawkey is the owner."[52] Eight years after Doby's integration of the senior circuit, Tom Yawkey's manager, Pinky Higgins, declared, "There'll be no niggers on this ball club as long as I have anything to say about it."[53] (Lacy wasn't far off in his assessment, although Higgins was eventually forced to relax his obstinate stance. Yawkey's Red Sox were the last major league team to integrate, adding Elijah "Pumpsie" Green to the club in 1959.)

A growing number of protests and demonstrations attempted to persuade the game's remaining all-white teams to relent. While some clubs, like the St. Louis Cardinals, loosely promised to bring a Black player aboard "in the near future," others, like Washington Senators owner Calvin Griffith, remained steadfast. "Nobody is going to stampede me into signing Negro players merely for the sake of satisfying certain pressure groups,"[54] Griffith said.

George Weiss of the New York Yankees was equally unbending: "[The Yankees] are averse to settling on a Negro player merely to meet the wishes of the people who insist they must have a Negro player."[55]

"We have been looking for a Negro player for some years," the New York general manager claimed. "We will have a Negro player as soon as we are able to find a Negro player among the availables."[56]

On November 30, 1952, Jackie Robinson appeared on the television program, *Youth Wants To Know*. As the show was coming to a close a young girl in the audience asked, "Mr. Robinson, do you think the Yankees are prejudiced against Negro players?"

Without hesitation Robinson replied, "Yes" stipulating that he wasn't referring to the players, who, in his words, were, "fine sportsmen and wonderful gentlemen."

But Jackie refused to excuse New York management. "There isn't a single Negro on the team now and there are very few in the entire Yankee farm system."

Robinson's charge certainly was not without merit. Weiss's true feelings were well known in baseball circles. "I will never allow a Black man to wear a Yankee uniform," Weiss was heard to say. "Box holders from Westchester don't want that sort of crowd. They would be offended to have to sit with niggers."[57]

Prejudice among the Yankee brain trust wasn't confined to the front office. As Robinson knew all too well from the many postseason matchups between his Dodgers and the Yankees, one of the most virulent bench jockeys was New York manager Casey Stengel.

"Nigger," "Jungle-bunny,"[58] and countless other epithets floated from Stengel's mouth to Robinson's ears.

"I'd get the usual—'nigger,' 'coon,' 'shoeshine,' 'boy,'" Larry Doby offered. 'I could understand from some fan or some jerk sitting on the bench. But I'd get it from managers too. Like Casey. He'd call me 'jig-a-boo.' But you mention this to the writers and they'd say, 'No, not Casey.'"

Neither Doby nor Robinson was surprised to learn of Stengel's analysis when the Yankees finally acquired a Black in 1955. "When I finally get a nigger,' Stengel said of Elston Howard, "I get the only one that can't run."[59]

On July 21, 1959, while mired in last place, the Boston Red Sox closed the books on baseball's apartheid when the signed Elijah "Pumsie" Green.

Jackie Robinson and Larry Doby had sparked a wildfire that spread even in the face of great resistance. The duo confirmed, beyond any shadow of doubt that Black men belonged in the major leagues. Doby and Robinson grasped their chance and spurred a revolution, their eyes firmly focused on the Prize.

"I thank God for giving me the ability and Mr. Veeck for giving me the opportunity," Doby said. "*All we ever asked for is an opportunity.*"[60]

4

Courage of Conviction: *Curt Flood*

"I do not feel that I am a piece of property to be bought and sold irrespective of my wishes. I believe that any system which produces that result violates my basic rights as a citizen and is inconsistent with the laws of the United States and of the several states."[1]

With this profound declaration, Curt Flood set in motion baseball's great financial revolution.

Curtis Charles Flood was born in Houston, Texas, on January 18, 1938. Before he reached the age of two, Flood's family had relocated to Oakland, California, where the economic prospects were much brighter.

Curt's parents worked countless hours to raise their family's standard of living. "We were not poor," Curt later explained, "but we had nothing. That is we ate at regular intervals, but not much."[2]

Flood recalled that he was in his teenage years before he learned that other families purchased a new Christmas tree every year. Herman Flood would ring in the yuletide season with a venture to the family basement where the previous year's tree hung upside down from a ceiling rafter, "to preserve the sap."[3] Three, and sometimes four, holiday seasons would pass before the elder Flood would replace the tree. Though the Floods could offer their children little in terms of personal possessions, they did, however, instill a belief in, and hope for, fulfillment of the American Dream.

"Every child in the grammar and junior high schools was Black," Curt recalled. "In the national tradition, the curriculum spared us the truth about our heritage. We had once been slaves, the teachers reminded; but now we were free. If anything went wrong, we had only ourselves to blame. Everybody rise and sing *Oh Beautiful for Spacious Skies*."[4]

Curt's cynicism would only strengthen in time.

As a child, Flood relished the opportunity to while his days away on the sandlots of Oakland. At the age of seven, Curt made a notable discovery: he had the innate ability to run faster than anyone in his neighborhood. Just a couple of years later, Curt realized he could throw and catch a baseball better than children more than twice his age. At nine, Curt joined a midget league club named Junior's Sweet Shop, a team coached by George Powles. Later, as coach at McClymonds High School, Powles developed a slew of professional athletes. In addition to Flood, Powles coached and tutored major leaguers, Joe Morgan, Frank Robinson, Vada Pinson, and Billy Martin; he also coached Bill Russell of the Boston Celtics, plus Ollie Matson and John Brodie of the National Football League.

Despite being a diminutive 5' 7" and 140 lbs, Flood still drew the interest of Cincinnati Reds scout Bobby Mattick. Though he was negotiating against himself, Mattick offered Curt $4,000 to sign with the Cincinnati organization for the 1956 season.

Ecstatic at the prospect of teaming up again with McClymonds schoolmate Frank Robinson, who had signed with the Reds a year earlier, Curt boarded a plane for Florida. Brimming with confidence, Flood was ready to take on the world; oblivious to the debasing conditions he would meet throughout his career.

Curt Flood's McClymonds teammate, Frank Robinson, reflected on the experience of many Latin Americans and African Americans who came from various points on the map when first confronted with the cultural realities of the American South. "I didn't know anything about racism or bigotry until I went into professional baseball in 1955.

"I had to ride in the back of buses, I could never find a Negro cab after games," Robinson wrote. "We had three Negroes on the team. We shared one small room in a boardinghouse without showers. We had to line up to get in the tub.... The Sally league was a hellhole for kids away from home for the first time, especially for kids who've had freedom like I had in Oakland. Segregation changes their character, hurts their personalities, and hinders their development."[5]

Robinson's name can be replaced with that of most any minority player coming up the through the minor league ranks in the Fifties and Sixties, and though the locale may vary, the plaint is similar.

Unlike Robinson, Flood had read all about Jim Crow and the separate facilities in Dixie. Nonetheless the actuality of discrimination that he witnessed when he arrived in Florida for his first spring training was unsettling. As he walked through the terminal toward the baggage claim, Curt noticed two water fountains. The drinking fountains were identical apart from the signs, which distinguished them as "White" and "Colored" respectively. This first hand confrontation with Southern segregation hit Flood, "like a door slammed in my face."[6]

Maybe, this illustration was something of an aberration, Curt thought; surely professional baseball would shelter him from this indignity. From the airport, Curt departed for the Floridian Hotel, the spring home of Cincinnati's Reds. Judging from the brochure the ball club had sent to him, the hotel certainly looked inviting; the high life of big time baseball awaited Curt.

He arrived at the team's hotel and confidently strode to the service desk. There, he informed the attendant that he was with the Reds, and that there should be a reservation for him under the name of Flood.

With a detached interest, the desk clerk turned away from Curt and shouted instructions to another hotel employee. An elderly Black porter knowingly came forward and waved to the perplexed Flood. Curt was escorted through the Flordian's lobby to the street, where a cab was hailed for the rookie.

"Ma Felder's," the porter instructed the driver.

A five-mile taxicab ride ensued, delivering Curt to the doorstep of Ma Felder's boarding house. There to greet Flood were Brooks Lawrence, Charlie Harmon, Joe Black, Pat Scantlebury and Frank Robinson. Comprising the Black contingent of the Cincinnati ball club, these men found themselves ostracized from their white teammates. Curt's idealism had been vanquished. The eighteen-year-old who emerged from that cab saw a lassitude in the eyes of his teammates. They had "the scars" of men who had been subjugated and wearied by the humiliation of segregation. Even before he donned a Reds uniform, Flood was indoctrinated into their "club."[7]

At the close of spring training Cincinnati dispatched Curt to their Carolina League affiliate, High Point-Thomasville. Professionally Curt was ready for the Carolina League, however, socially, the southern community was not ready for him.

"Black bastard," "Eight ball," "Sno-ball," and "jigaboo"[8] were among the wide variety of racist taunts that were heaped upon Curt, not just at his home ballpark, but also throughout the Carolina League. Even under the torrent of abuse, Flood could not turn to his teammates for solace. The presence of a Black man on their team was as offensive to the members of the club as it was to the surrounding community.

Curt later remembered that his teammates ostracized him, refusing to even speak to him off the diamond. His manager offered no support, verbally or emotionally. The eighteen-year-old was left to fend for himself with no guidance or encouragement forthcoming from anyone in his own clubhouse.

Alienated from his teammates, Flood would return to the sanctuary of his motel room and break down. "I felt too young for the ordeal," Curt said. "I wanted to be free of these animals whose fifty cent bleacher ticket was a license to curse my color and deny my humanity. I wanted to be free of the imbeciles on the ball team."[9]

His teammates looked upon him as "subhuman," Curt later reported. On more than one occasion during that trying season Flood harbored thoughts of purposely striking out so "our cracker pitcher would lose another game."[10] With similar motivation, he also pondered dropping a fly ball, or committing a throwing error.

Curt never followed through with his seditious designs. Instead, he threw himself headlong into the game, determined to prove his worth to his detractors. Bill White, a future Cardinal teammate of Flood's, worked through similar frustration in much the same fashion. While playing for the Giants Danville, Virginia team, White was the sole Black in the Carolina League in 1952. Raised a world away from Dixie in Warren, Ohio, White was unprepared for the discrimination and hate that the unique circumstance provided.

"I yelled back at the name callers," White admitted. "I was only eighteen and immature. The more the fans gave it to me, the harder I hit the ball.... They eventually decided to leave me alone, which was a victory over bigotry."[11]

White lashed back, but other players, like Willie Stargell, suffered in silence. "Like a pain in my pelvis," Stargell wrote in his autobiography, "it was a constant source of pain, but I never spoke to anyone about it."[12]

Philadelphia farmhand Dick Allen endured more than most African Americans during his minor league career. The first Black to play in Little Rock, Arkansas, Allen was saluted by the Traveler faithful. "When I arrived at the park, there were people marching around outside with signs," Allen said. "One said, 'DON'T NEGRO-IZE BASEBALL.' Another, ' NIGGER GO HOME.' ... Here, in my mind, I thought Jackie Robinson had 'Negro-ized baseball sixteen years earlier."[13]

Commissioner Ford Frick, comfortably seated in his New York office, was blissfully oblivious to Dick Allen's turmoil. "The local folks expected trouble," Frick said of the integration of the Arkansas Travelers. "On opening day the park was picketed, by just one man. The next day the one-man picket line failed to show, and he has never been seen since. And colored players now play there in every game without any problems whatsoever."[14]

Throwing out the first ball at Allen's initial contest was Arkansas governor Orville Faubus who just a few years earlier declared, "I will never open public schools as integrated institutions." Perhaps the governor's presence was fitting, for following the game Allen walked to his car where he found a letter on his windshield. The note said, 'DON'T COME BACK AGAIN NIGGER.' Allen looked around and realized he was alone in the parking lot.

"There might be something more terrifying than being Black and holding a note that says 'NIGGER' in an empty parking lot in Little Rock, Arkansas, in 1963," Allen told writer Tim Whitaker, "but if there is, it hasn't crossed my path yet."[15]

At least one player can relate an equally surreal tale. For two decades, Stargell kept to himself a threat that was made on his life while he was playing for Pittsburgh's Plainview, Texas, farm team. The caveat was delivered as Willie made his way to the ball yard on foot.

"A white man, hiding around a corner, jumped into my path," Stargell explained in his memoirs. "He had a shotgun in his hand. The next thing I felt was the cold metal barrels of the gun pressed tightly against my temple. Though I began to shake like a leaf, the gun-bearing bigot never flinched. He was as calm as a walk through the park.

"Nigger, if you play in that game tonight, I'll blow your brains out."[16] Stargell, with weak knees, did play that evening, jumping each time he heard a car backfire.

The threat of violence often loomed over these groundbreaking players, regardless of their locale. Henry Aaron recalled his experience while integrating the South Atlantic League. "We heard some catcalls all around the league," Aaron wrote in *Baseball Has Done It.* "We played in towns like Savannah, Macon, and Montgomery. We got catcalls and people threatening us in letters in Montgomery. They'd write they were coming out to the ballpark and sit in right field with a rifle and shoot us. We got all sorts of threats, but it didn't worry me. I was there to play baseball, that was the only thing I was concerned with."[17]

With an astounding sense of purpose, these men were able to perform, and excel, on the playing field. Nary a soul of them would have been required to justify their actions had they bolted from their club and fled the abuse. Across the board, though, this generation of Black players was determined to assert their worth. If they weren't accepted off the field, they were determined to prove their worth on the diamond ... a giant step toward actual equality.

Magnifying the accomplishments of these men is baseball's complete lack of thought and concern for the well being of their ballplayers. Inexplicably, but not really surprisingly, given the game's track record, management turned a blind eye to the troubles facing their young prospects. It may have been ignorance, or simply a complete lack of regard; but there is no reasonable defense of the cavalier attitude displayed when baseball desegregated its minor leagues.

Commissioner Frick proffered the absurd notion that organized baseball, in the course of desegregating its various leagues, was an admirable, no *exceptional*, illustration of how integration could peaceably be accomplished.

"I think baseball offers a terrific example of how this kind of resentment, these objections, can be handled. There's a great lesson to be learned in how we've handled the problem,"[18] Frick said.

Dick Allen articulated the feelings of his contemporaries when he wrote, "Maybe if the Phillies had called me in, man to man, like the Dodgers had done with Jackie, and said, 'Dick this is what we have in mind, it's going to be very difficult, but we're with you'—at least then I would have been prepared. I'm not saying I would have liked it. But I *would* have known what to expect."[19]

El Birdos

Flood's time spent with the Cincinnati organization was short. The Reds tried to convert him into a third baseman, forty-one errors later, the Cincinnati management decided Flood was better suited to be an outfielder *in St. Louis.*

Had Curt remained in Cincinnati, the Reds would have had an all McClymonds (not to mention an all-Black) outfield. Following Robinson and Flood to Cincinnati was Vada Pinson, another McClymonds alumnus. The Reds adhered to the game's conventional thinking of the day, and opted against an all-Black outfield, regardless of the trio's talent level.

While playing winter ball in Latin America following the '57 season, Curt received a wire from Cincinnati's general manager Gabe Paul. He had been traded to the St. Louis Cardinals. "The Reds wished me luck," Curt said. "Hail and Farwell."[20]

The Cardinal ball club that Flood joined was similar to most major league teams of the late Fifties: two distinct and separate factions within one entity; Black and white. The team's clubhouse, like the city of St. Louis itself, was Jim Crow. Under manager Solly Hemus (dubbed "Little Faubus" by pitcher Bennie Daniels, in honor of Arkansas' governor), Flood and his Black teammates languished and struggled to reach their full potential.

Intuitively, with the instinct only possessed by a man who had felt the slights of bigotry, Flood believed that Hemus was offended by his presence. Curt's evidence was circumstantial, but heartfelt. Hemus avoided all personal contact with the ballplayer, and spoke with Flood only out of necessity.

The Redbird manager also had a distinct distaste for pitcher Bob Gibson. Hemus shuttled Gibson back and forth between the bullpen and the starting rotation, and then back and forth between the parent club and the minor leagues.

If Gibson and Flood had any doubts about Hemus's open-mindedness, they were put to rest following a 1960 contest against the Pirates. In that game, the Cardinal player/manager inserted himself into the game as a pinch hitter. On the mound for Pittsburgh was former Redbird Bennie Daniels. With the first pitch, Daniels knocked Hemus down. Following the second delivery Hemus swung, missed, and let his bat go towards the mound. The next pitch plunked "Little Faubus" in the back. On the way towards first base, Hemus had several choice words for the Pittsburgh mounds-man.

The following day the Cardinal manager called his team together.

"I want you to be the first to know what I said to Daniels yesterday," Hemus said to his charges. "I called him a black son of a bitch."

"End of statement," Flood stated. "End of meeting. Not one word of regret.... We had been wondering how the manager felt about us, and now we knew. Now we hated him for himself. We became more discerning in our evaluations of baseball employment policies;... we saw more clearly than before that Black players of less than star quality tended to disappear from the scene in a few years, whereas mediocre whites hung on long enough to qualify for pensions: In baseball, as elsewhere, the Black had to be better than a white of equal experience, or he would be shown the door."[21]

Midway through the '61 season conditions improved for Black Cardinals, if not for African Americans across baseball as a whole. "Managers," the old saying goes, " are hired to be fired." Mercifully, Hemus adhered to this unwritten baseball rule, and a new, player friendly regime arrived with Solly's replacement, Johnny Keane.

The new St. Louis pilot knew Curt well having already coached him during Flood's stay with the Cardinals' Omaha affiliate.

Playing under Keane, Curt and his teammates flourished. The Cardinals promptly became a *team* in the truest sense of the term. An important transition had occurred. Johnny Keane didn't consider a man's color when fielding a team. He simply filled out his line-up card with the names of the best nine available to him. On Keane's first day in command he assured Curt that the centerfield job was his, an assurance that did much to buttress Flood's confidence.

Keane's refreshing outlook instilled a new spirit into a club that had repeatedly failed to live up to its promise. The recently integrated spring training conditions (1961) played a large part in boosting team morale. Men who previously went their separate ways following a game's conclusion were suddenly surprised to find themselves enjoying each other's company.

Curt Flood, "the best centerfielder in baseball" (© Bettmann/CORBIS).

"We had cookouts every night and the players got to know each other, the wives were together and the kids all played together,"[22] Bill White reported. In short order the Cardinals became baseball's first truly integrated ball club, on and off the field.

"The Cardinals were the rare team that not only believed in each other but genuinely *liked* other." Gibson said. "We'd go out to eat after a ball game and a dozen guys would show up, Black and white."[23]

Everything fell into place for the Redbirds in 1964. With an infectious sense of camaraderie, and a skipper who inspired the faith of his players, the Cardinals marched to a National League pennant. St. Louis captured their first world championship in eighteen years when they defeated the New York Yankees in that season's fall classic.

Johnny Keane resigned following the world title and was replaced by Red Schoendienst. Red's easygoing style resulted in two more pennants in '67 and '68. A World Series victory against Boston in 1967 was followed by a seven game defeat at the hands of the Detroit Tigers one year later.

Simultaneous with the Cardinals' run as the National League's finest club, Curt Flood had developed into arguably the best centerfielder in baseball. While earning seven Gold Gloves for his fielding excellence, Curt set a major league record of 396 chances and 226 consecutive games without an error. His skill with the glove merited Curt the prestigious honor of being a 1968 cover subject for *Sports Illustrated*. "The Best Centerfielder in Baseball,"[24] the sports weekly proclaimed of Flood, an opinion that was held by a number of other observers.

"Flood's the greatest outfielder around now," Dodger catcher John Roseboro said, "even better than Willie Mays."[25] Curt was no slouch at the plate either, as his career average of .293 and a lifetime total of 1,861 hits will attest.

The window of opportunity for a ballplayer to capture his maximum reward is relatively small. A number of Cardinals, Flood included, sought higher compensation in the wake of their mini-dynasty. Players for a two-time pennant winning ball club will, quite understandably, seek higher recompense for their services. When his star players asked for an increase in pay for the upcoming '69 campaign, August Busch, beer baron and proprietor of baseball's St. Louis Cardinals, exploded.

Lou Brock, Bob Gibson, Tim McCarver, Flood, and several of their teammates requested, and ultimately received, higher wages. Busch was beside himself about these ingrates. "These players cared only for themselves and to hell with the fans,"[26] Gussie crowed, taking up the mantle for the paying customer and (beer) consumer. He and all his multi-millions were for the "little guy," and these greedy men cared nary an iota for "Joe six-pack." This notion, coupled with the Major League Player's Association request of its members to refrain from signing their individual contracts until the game's owners agreed to a better retirement plan, angered the game's powerbrokers. When the Player's Association and management reached a compromise, Gussie's players had the audacity to seek their personal raises.

The Cardinal owner called a special meeting on March 22 in St. Petersburg where he would vent his boiled-over hostility. Knowing his players had no option but to sit and listen to his rambling diatribe, Busch filled the air with the petty and unreasonable complaints of a man who failed to recognize a changing time.

"True, you deserve to be well paid in accordance with your playing ability," Busch said. "But I must call your attention to the fact of life that you take few, if any, of the great risks involved.

"Fans are telling us now that if we intend to raise prices to pay for the high salaries and so on and on, they will stop coming to the games, they will not watch and will not listen. They say they can do other things with their time and with their money."[27]

Busch's rant left his club dispirited. The belief among Cardinal players was that their two successive pennants meant nothing; the owner had put them in their place. Who were they to expect raises on merit? They should be grateful for the opportunity that he, the Cardinals and major league baseball was providing them.

Nineteen sixty-nine was a disappointing season for the defending National League champs. Flood became convinced that Cardinal management was "sabotaging" the club's chances of repeating their previous success. Several questionable personnel changes angered the players, including the trade that sent Orlando Cepeda to Atlanta for Joe Torre.

"They've already sold a million and half tickets this season," Curt complained, "so they can well afford to prevent us from having good years. Wait and see how they rub it in at contract time next winter."[28]

Flood was too vocal; he was too opinionated for members of the Cardinal's front office. In his heart, Curt knew that his days with St. Louis were numbered. Player trades are not unusual in the world of baseball. Men are shuttled between teams much the way bonds are bartered on Wall Street. Professional baseball players, though idolized by the masses, are little more than property to their "owners," chattel to be shuffled back and forth between various franchises.

Most assuredly, a malcontent, as Flood was perceived to be, would be dealt away at the earliest possible date. Following the '69 season, which saw Curt bat .285, slightly under his career average, Flood was sitting in his apartment when his phone rang.

"Hello Curt," said a voice that would identify itself as Jim Toomey, an assistant to the Cardinal general manager. "Curt, you've been traded to Philadelphia."

A stunned Flood responded with silence, a quiet that was broken by the junior Cardinal executive "You, McCarver, Hoener and Byron Brone, for Richie Allen, Cookie Rojas and Jerry Johnson," Toomey informed Flood.

"Good luck, Curt."

Though rationally Flood understood the trade, especially in the wake of events of the previous months, he was nonetheless shocked by the actual transaction. "*Twelve years of my life*", he thought to himself.

"There ain't no way I'm going to pack up and move twelve years of my life away from here," Curt ominously told a friend. "No way at all."[29]

I Won't Stand for It

A student of the game, Curt well understood the place that player trades had in the sport. Nevertheless, the transaction rankled with Flood. "If I had been a foot-shuffling porter, they might have at least given me a pocket watch," Curt wrote. "But all I got was a call from a middle-echelon coffee drinker in the front office."[30]

Flood weighed his options. He could go to Philadelphia, a town he considered rife with prejudice, or he could quit. He began telling reporters that he would choose the latter option and retire from the game, but he could not shake the inherent unfairness of in the game's inflexibility.

Curt refused to allow the game to treat him like a piece of property. He had established a life in St. Louis and now he was being told to relocate to Philadelphia with no questions asked. "They shoot down my rights," Flood told a friend. "They shoot me down as a man. I won't stand for it."[31]

Rule 9 of the Major League rules provided, in part: "A club may assign to another club an existing contract with a player. The player, upon receipt of written notice of such assignments, is by his contract bound to serve the assignee."[32] This is the "reserve clause."

For Flood to challenge the validity of the Cardinals right to reassign his contract to Philadelphia, he would have to attack baseball's reserve clause. To render the reserve clause obsolete, Flood would have to beat baseball in the court system. In order to sue the game, it would behoove Curt to receive the backing of the Player's Association. Curt flew to New York where he met with Marvin Miller, the lead counsel for the Association.

Flood informed Miller that he wanted to sue baseball and test the legality of the reserve system in a court of law. "I want to go out like a man instead of disappearing like a bottle cap,"[33] he explained.

Miller was impressed with Flood, but still wanted the outfielder to seriously consider the repercussions should he follow through on his threat to sue baseball. A lawsuit would surely last two or three years, Miller cautioned, and at thirty-one, Curt only had several prime earning years left in his career.

Despite all of Miller's warnings, Flood remained adamant, "You haven't begun to scare me yet. Let's sue."[34]

To obtain support from the Player's Association, Flood would have to convince the Executive Board. Miller invited Curt to appear in San Juan on December 13 to speak before the player representatives.

Following a thirty-minute talk by Flood, during which he explained his position, the various player reps peppered Curt with questions.

Was he just doing this as a negotiating ploy? Was Curt hoping to milk a few extra dollars out of Philadelphia?

"I can't be bought," Flood sternly told the meeting.

Tom Haller of the Los Angeles Dodgers then spoke up. "This is a period of Black militants," Hall stated, "Do you feel you're doing this as a part of that movement? Because you're Black?"

Though the question surprised Marvin Miller, Flood was unmoved. "All the things you say are true," he concurred. "And I'd be lying if I told you that as a Black man in baseball I hadn't gone through worse times than my teammates. I'll also say, yes, I think the change in Black consciousness in recent years has made me more sensitive to injustice in every area of my life. But I want you to know that what I'm doing here I'm doing as a ballplayer, a major league ballplayer, and I think it's absolutely terrible that we have stood by and watched this situation go on for so many years and never pulled together to do anything about it. It's improper, it shouldn't be allowed to go any further, and the circumstances are such that, well, I guess this is the time to do something about it."[35]

Say It Loud...

> If there is no struggle, there is no progress.... Power concedes nothing without demand. It never did and it never will.
>
> Frederick Douglas[36]

"I'm a child of the sixties," Curt Flood said upon reflection. "I'm a man of the sixties." To understand Flood, his pride, his conviction, one must take a survey of his era.

"During that period of time this country was coming apart at the seams. We were in Southeast Asia... Good men were dying for America and the Constitution. In the southern part of the United States we were marching for civil rights, and to think that merely because I was a professional baseball player, I could ignore what was going on outside the walls of Busch Stadium [was] truly hypocrisy and now I found that all of those rights that these great Americans were dying for, I didn't have in my own profession."[37]

Curt had long been politically aware, educating himself on issues and lending his time to progressive causes. In the early sixties Flood moved to the forefront of the movement when, along with Jackie Robinson and pugilists Floyd Patterson and Archie Moore, he traveled to Jackson, Mississippi in 1963. There the sporting heroes attended a banquet and delivered speeches to boost the morale of civil rights activists and volunteers who were working in a most hostile environment. In Jackson Curt met with the NAACP's field representative in Mississippi, Medgar Evers. Evers had spearheaded the NAACP's push to desegregate public facilities in Mississippi and enforce the 1954 Supreme Court ruling *Brown v Board of Education of Topeka, Kansas.*

"Segregated schools are not equal and cannot be made equal and hence they are deprived of equal protection of the laws,"[38] Chief Justice Warren said, as he read the Court's May 17, 1954 decision. This ruling overturned *Plessy v Ferguson,* an 1896 Supreme Court ruling that deemed separate, but equal, was Constitutional — the legal basis for Jim Crow laws.

Brown was undoubtedly the most important step since the Emancipation Proclamation in securing the civil liberties of all Americans.

In Flood remembered that the 1954 decision provoked "little discussion, and no excitement"[39] in his hometown.

Despite the high court's ruling outlawing segregation, Jim Crow was slow in dying. For the St. Louis Cardinals, separate accommodations were still required during their spring training residency in Florida. The separate and decidedly unequal living conditions had long been a sore point with Black members of the Cardinals. Flood, fully understanding the ramifications of *Brown*, had been the leader of a group of Redbirds whose patience with the status quo had worn thin.

In 1960, Curt approached St. Louis general manager Bing Devine and expressed his discomfort with the spring training conditions he and his Black teammates endured in Jim Crow Florida.

Devine offered Flood no solace, segregation, after all, was the law in Florida.

Perhaps, Curt offered, the club should select another locale to train. The general manager, however, shot down his suggestion. The Cardinals would remain in Florida. They would stay in the same proximity where other teams trained, where they had a substantial investment in their training facilities, where segregation still ruled.

While Flood and his Black teammates were staying "across the tracks," in the Black section of St. Petersburg, their white counterparts lived in a first class hotel. Some Redbirds even rented beachfront homes and invited their families down for the Florida stay, evolving spring training into a paid vacation.

"The house where we lived was owned by a woman who charged us each $49 a week and provided a couple of meals a day," Flood's roommate, Bob Gibson, remembered. "It was a shame ... and a terrible disappointment. I had traveled more than 2,000 miles and I still had not escaped the ghetto."

"So this," Gibson thought to himself, "is the major leagues."[40]

Contrasting with Gibson's account was Robert Boyle of *Sports Illustrated*: "St. Louis Negro players live in a comfortably rented house in the colored section of St. Petersburg."[41] Though Boyle viewed the Cardinals' surroundings as satisfactory, to Gibson and his comrades the situation was degrading and humiliating. Still, despite the derogatory circumstances, Black and Latino players thrived on the playing field.

Rounding third and heading for home was a *Brown Eyed Handsome* man. A new day had dawned, and Chuck Berry, through his hero/protagonist, served to document this insurgency.

Pumpsie Green's arrival in Boston in 1959 had completed baseball's excruciatingly slow integration process. However, Black dominance in the game was under way well before the Red Sox reluctantly added a player of color to their roster. The arrival of Blacks in organized ball drastically altered the strategy of the game. Players such as Henry Aaron, Willie Mays and Frank Robinson, possessed power and speed, an exciting combination that began a new age. From Jackie's debut in 1947 until 1970, Black players captured 17 batting crowns, 10 home run titles, and 19 Most Valuable Player awards.

"If there's a single reason why the Black players of the 1950s and 1960s were so much better than the white players," Aaron wrote in *I Had A Hammer*, "I believe it's because we had to be. And we knew we had to be. There was too much at stake for us to screw it up. Black people had been crying out for opportunity in this country for two centuries, and finally we had it. Our mission- and that's the only thing to call it- was to do something with the chance we had."[42]

Opportunity was at hand, but equality off the field remained out of reach. Fortified by their own ability, and empowered by an undeniable sense of self worth, African Americans were weary of second-class citizenship. The irony for many Black ball players lay in the fact that their superiority on the ball field failed to translate into respect away from the diamond.

"I probably can not influence those whites who complain that they are tired of feeling guilty about what their grandfather did to my grandfather," Flood wrote, "but I can at least suggest that they stop making idiotic comparisons between my people and European immigrants. I think it wholesome to bear in mind that American statute and unlegislated custom not only enslaved my people, but also outlawed their language, their religion, and their expressions of group and individual dignity. Including their desire to form abiding family relationships. They were bred like cattle. It is inspiring that so many survived with their finer feelings intact, after a century of emancipation in which color has been badge of ineligibility. *To hell with your grandfather baby. Just get out of the way.*"[43]

> Revolutions are never compromising. Revolutions are not based upon any kind of tokenism whatsoever. Revolutions are never even based upon that which is begging a corrupt system to accept us into it. Revolutions overturn systems.
>
> Malcolm X, "The Black Revolution," 4/8/64[44]

On October 16, 1968, six days after Detroit's World Series victory over the Cardinals, two Olympians representing the United States made a symbolic protest that jarred the nation and the world. From the awards podium where they received their respective gold and bronze medals, Tommy Smith and John Carlos each raised a black-gloved fist during the playing of the *Star Spangled Banner*. From Mexico City, this silent, effective demonstration emboldened a growing Black-power movement at home.

"The Black fist in the air was only in recognition of those who had gone," Carlos explained. "It was a prayer of solidarity, it was a cry for help by my fellow brothers and sisters in this country. Who had been lynched, who had been shot, who had hoses turned on them ... a cry for freedom."[45]

Carlos and Smith, with their heads bowed, and their clinched fists held aloft towards the heavens, silently called to mind activists who had passed before.

On December 1, 1955, Rosa Parks, returning home from her job at Montgomery Fair department store, refused to yield her seat on the bus to a white man, thereby imbedding her name in our nation's conscience. More than a decade earlier, on July 6, 1944, Lt. Jack Robinson would not obey an order to leave his seat and move to the back of the bus in which he was riding. Robinson was steadfast in his refusal to accede to the command: "No, I'm not going to move to the back of the bus," Robinson said to the driver. "You had better sit down and drive the bus wherever you are going."[46]

For his determined stance Robinson was court-martialed by the Army, but not even the U.S. Government could dampen Jackie's spirit. Robinson brought this fiery determination with him to the major leagues, and enlivened an entire race. The vision of a Black on a baseball diamond, on equal footing with his white contemporaries, was compelling to a community long oppressed. Black America sat riveted to the radio, to news reports, and in the grandstands, breathlessly awaiting Jackie's latest exploit. Robinson, Doby, and other groundbreaking Blacks in the game stirred an enormous sense of hope and optimism. Robinson represented more than a flannel clad, ball-playing troubadour, Jackie promoted racial pride.

"Sport," Dr. Harry Edwards has observed, "was a legitimate lever to bring about changes relative to race. A battle for dignity and respect."[47]

Playing with unrestrained desire, Robinson used baseball as a vehicle to disprove any notion of racial inferiority. For all of his groundbreaking, however, Robinson never attempted to shatter baseball's backbone, the reserve system.

On December 24, 1969, Flood informed baseball's new commissioner Bowie Kuhn that he was challenging the game's reserve clause.

Dear Mr. Kuhn:

After twelve years in the major leagues, I do not feel that I am a piece of property to be bought and sold irrespective of my wishes. I believe that any system which produces that result violates my basic rights as a citizen and is inconsistent with the laws of the United States and of the several States.

It is my desire to play baseball in 1970, and I am capable of playing. I have received a contract offer from the Philadelphia club, but I believe I have the right to consider offers from other clubs before making any decisions. I, therefore, request that you make known to all Major League clubs my feelings in this matter, and advise them of my availability for the 1970 season.[48]

"There came that moment when I had to drop that letter in the mailbox," Flood said later, "and I felt this fear, a fear instilled in every player through all those years by the very, very clever men who ran baseball. After I mailed the letter, there was a second wave of uneasiness, a fear of the unknown, because I had no idea how this would work out. But then came a feeling of relief that, finally, somebody was doing something about the problem in the game."[49]

Six days later a reply was in the mail, the leaders of the game had no intention of addressing "the problem in the game."

"Dear Curt," read Kuhn's informal, and disrespectful, salutation.

"I certainly agree with you that you, as a human being, are not a piece of property to be bought and sold. That is fundamental in our society and I think obvious. However, I cannot see its applicability to the situation at hand.

"You have entered into a current playing contract since 1956. Your present contract has been assigned in accordance with its provisions by the St. Louis club to the Philadelphia club. The provisions of the playing contract have been negotiated over the years between the clubs and the players, most recently when the present basic agreement was negotiated two years ago between the clubs and the Player's Association... Under the circumstances, and pending any further information from you, I do not comply with the request contained in the second paragraph of your letter."[50]

On January 16 former Supreme Court Justice Arthur Goldberg, representing Curt Flood, filed suit in New York Federal Court. Goldberg's aim was to nullify the transaction between St. Louis and Philadelphia and therefore make Flood a free agent. More important to the Player's Association as a whole, that decision would terminate the reserve clause as a violation of U.S. anti-trust laws.

Notification of the suit sent a panic through the game's hierarchy. Joe Cronin and Warren Giles, the American and National League presidents, issued a joint statement warning that, "professional baseball would simply cease to exist" if Goldberg and Flood succeeded in annihilating the reserve system.

As presidents of the two major leagues we regret that Curt Flood, a highly paid star who has contributed much to and obtained much from baseball, has decided to refuse to honor the assignment of his contract by the St. Louis Cardinals to the Philadelphia Phillies and has demanded that he be permitted to play major league baseball where he pleases.

When a player refuses to honor an assignment he violates a contract in which he agrees that assignments may be made and he violates the fundamental baseball rules, including the reserve clause, which experience has shown to be absolutely necessary to the successful operation of baseball. [51]

A seven-point argument by the league presidents explained why the game would be laid bare should the reserve clause be abolished.

"Without the reserve clause, the wealthier clubs could sign an unbeatable club of All-Stars, totally destroying league competition," Cronin and MacPhail claimed.

"The integrity of the game would be threatened as players could negotiate with one club while playing for another."[52]

The reserve clause gave an individual club the rights to a player in perpetuity. Each standard player's contract stipulated that the player was obligated for the year signed, and the club held an option for another year. Paragraph 10A of the Uniform Player's Contract stated, "The club shall have the right to renew this contract for the period of one year on the same terms."

Justice Oliver Wendell Holmes declared baseball exempt from antitrust laws in his May 29, 1922, opinion: "the business (baseball) is the giving of exhibition games, which are purely state matters." Despite several attacks on that 1922 ruling, baseball still possessed that exempt status when Flood brought his suit. To succeed, Flood would have to prove that baseball was not sacrosanct, that, indeed, the sport was nothing more than a business, no different than any other.

"To challenge the sanctity of organized baseball was to question one of the primary myths of the American culture,"[53] Curt wrote.

Flood's suit was not the first attempt to challenge the legality of baseball's "Rock of Gilbralter." In 1953, a New York Yankees farmhand, George Toolson, challenged the tenets of the basic contract. Unable to make the World Champion parent club, Toolson found himself buried in New York's minor league system. Toolson wanted the opportunity to reach the major leagues with another club; the Yankees instead opted to keep him indefinitely as indemnity against injury on the big league club.

Toolson's suit against baseball for violating antitrust laws reached the U.S. Supreme Court. Despite the Court's previous ruling that the sports of football, boxing and horse racing were all subject to antitrust laws, they found against Toolson. "Right or wrong, we exempt baseball from the antitrust laws," the majority opinion read. "That's the precedent. If the Congress thinks that is an error, it can change the decision by legislation."[54]

Flood's suit was brought before Judge Irving Ben Cooper, of the U.S. District Court's for the Southern District of New York.

A number of prominent men in the sport agreed with the principle that Curt was arguing. None of his backers meant more to Flood than Jackie Robinson. Robinson recognized that money wasn't the issue at the heart of Flood's argument: Basic human rights lay at the core of Curt's quest.

"I think Curt is doing a service to all players in the leagues," Robinson said, "especially for the younger players coming up who are not superstars. All he is asking is the right to negotiate. It doesn't surprise me that he had the courage to do it. He's a very sensitive man concerned about the rights of everybody. We need men of integrity like Curt Flood and Bill Russell who are involved in the area of civil rights, and who are not willing to let Mr. Charlie dictate their needs and wants for them."[55]

Such encouragement went far in fortifying Curt as he prepared for litigation. Still, as was expected, all did not hail Flood's actions. Various houseboys spoke up to recite the establishment line, including Red Sox

Curt Flood: "I don't feel that I am a piece of property to be bought and sold irrespective of my wishes" (© Bettman/CORBIS).

star Carl Yastrzemski, who believed the Player's Association should not support Flood's suit.

At trial, a number of company men took the stand in defense of baseball and the reserve clause. Bing Devine, Joe Cronin, Chub Feeney, John McCale and Joe Garagiola, among others, all testified on behalf of major league baseball.

Robinson, Hank Greenberg, former owner Bill Veeck and Marvin Miller supported Flood's contention under oath. More than any other witness, Robinson's presence in the courtroom lingered in Flood's mind's eye.

The proceedings took place before an attentive packed house. In the midst of testimony the courtroom doors swung open and in strode a familiar figure. Though aged and slowed by recent illness, all in attendance still instantly recognized Jackie Robinson. The former baseball great slowly walked down the aisle and found a seat near an incredulous Flood.

"I never called him," said Curt. "I wouldn't dare. He just volunteered, showed up on his own, and he told us he wanted to take the stand and describe what it was like for a ballplayer.... Then he finished and left the stand and walked out of that room and every eye was on him."[56]

"I can't see how modifying the reserve clause in any way could affect the game in a derogatory manner," Robinson said from the stand. "I think it would improve in terms of the relationship between owners and players and I think basically this is what we are after: to have a better relationship between management and players if you are to have a great game.

"Anything that is one sided is wrong. The reserve clause is one-sided in favor of the owners and should be modified to give the player some control over his own destiny. If the reserve clause is not modified, I think you will have a serious strike by the players."[57]

"Everyone," Bill Veeck testified, " should have the right, at least once, to determine his future."[58]

From the stand the maverick Veeck offered a solution, his "Hollywood" plan, modeled after an arrangement that had existed for years between studios and actors. "I wanted to put into effect an equity-type contract calling for scheduled raises, and scheduled option periods. If a player didn't sign, he became a free agent at the end of seven years...."[59]

In contrast, lawyers for baseball argued that the abolishment of the reserve clause would alter the game beyond recognition. The better players would switch clubs every year, traveling wherever the highest offer lay. The game's wealthy franchises would monopolize the best talent; to which Goldberg responded that this was simply capitalism in action.

The owner's reluctance to modify the reserve clause even a little was made abundantly clear at a 1970 meeting between player representatives and baseball officials. Jim Bouton, a pitcher for the Houston Astros, facetiously asked if the reserve clause could be terminated when a player reached the age of sixty-five.

"No," National League attorney Lou Carrol answered, "because the next time you'll want it reduced to fifty-five."[60]

To no one's surprise, Cooper did not rule against the owners. The judge, moreover, showed obvious distain for the plaintiff during the course of the trial. Cooper, according to Marvin Miller, "baited" Flood on the stand.

"This isn't as easy as playing centerfield, is it?"[61] the jurist said to Flood.

The judge did not rule on the merits of Flood's argument, instead Cooper relied on the previous high court decision that gave major league baseball immunity from anti-trust laws.

"Prior to the trial, we gained the impression that there was a view held by many that baseball's reserve system had occasioned rampant abuse and that it should be abolished.

"We were struck by the fact, however, that the testimony at trial failed to support that criticism; we find no general or widespread disregard of the extremely important position the player occupies.

"Clearly the preponderance of credible proof does not favor elimination of the reserve clause.... Under the existing rules of baseball, by refusing to report to Philadelphia the plaintiff is, by his own act, foreclosing himself from continuing a professional baseball career, a consequence to be deplored. Nevertheless, he has the right to retire and embark upon a different enterprise outside organized baseball....

"Baseball has been the National Pastime for over one hundred years and enjoys a unique place in our American Heritage," Cooper said. "Major League professional baseball is avidly followed by millions of fans, looked upon with fervor and pride and provides a special source of inspiration and competitive team spirit especially for the young.

"Baseball's status in the life of the nation is so persuasive that it would not strain credulity to say the court can take judicial notice that baseball is everybody's business. To put it mildly and with restraint, it would be unfortunate indeed if a fine sport and profession, which brings surcease from daily travail and an escape from the ordinary to most inhabitants of this land, were to suffer in the least because of undue concentration by any one or any group on commercial and profit considerations. The game is on higher ground; it behooves everyone to keep it here."[62]

To think that a man who thus canonized the game would rule fairly might be expecting too much and Cooper did not disappoint. The Judge refused to sully the fine American institution. Curt's next option would be Federal Appeals Court, where, as expected, the three-man court upheld Cooper's ruling leaving Flood with one remaining option, the Supreme Court.

As the winter of 1970-'71 approached, Curt found himself financially strapped. His painting and photographic studio had gone bust, and personal expenses were mounting as each day passed. At the close of the 1970 season, Washington Senators owner Bob Short approached Flood about the possibility of playing for his club the following summer. Economically Curt had little choice but to consider the offer, but the foremost thought in his mind was the implications of any such agreement for the pending litigation. After receiving firm assurances from his lawyers and Marvin Miller that his lawsuit would not be affected should he reach a contractual understanding with the Senators, Flood entered negotiations with Short.

A trade was consummated between Washington and Philadelphia, who still retained the rights to Flood. The Senators parted with three nondescript prospects in exchange for the right to negotiate with Flood. Included in the deal for Curt were Greg Goosen, Gene Martin, and Jeff Terpko. Flood and Short agreed to a one-year, $110,000 contract, but not before the two sides embarked upon lengthy, and complicated, negotiations. Flood's attorneys insisted that the contract contain three points.

1. Curt's pay would not be cut regardless of what happened during the season.
2. He would not be traded without his consent.
3. He would become a free agent if he and the Senators could not agree to a contract for the 1972 season.

Though Short was willing to comply with all three requests, Bowie Kuhn was adamant in his refusal to allow any deviation from the standard player contract.

"I made it perfectly clear to both Flood and Short that there would be no agreements beyond the standard contract," the commissioner firmly declared. "If they made oral agreements, they would be unenforceable. All baseball contracts are clear: that any provisions not written into the contracts are not binding."[63]

Despite Kuhn's saber rattling, Short and Flood made a handshake agreement. "If he played for me past June 15 he'd be paid for the full season, which I always do," Short reasoned. "If he had a terrible year and hit .100 and couldn't field or throw, I couldn't trade him anyway, because who'd want a 33 year-old outfielder like that at $110,000 anyway. And if we couldn't agree on 1972, there was no way I could farm him out or trade him, either."[64]

Short was convinced that the agreement wouldn't "in any way" impinge on the reserve clause. " It just recognizes that Flood is a human being."[65]

In a far more benevolent world, Curt Flood would have returned from his year in exile and recaptured his playing brilliance of days past. Regrettably, Curt's sabbatical had allowed the erosion of his skills, to say nothing of the deterioration in his mental health. Just thirteen games into his Washington Senators career, Curt jumped the club.

"I tried," Flood said in a wire to Bob Short; " a year and a half is too much. Very serious problems mounting every day. Thank you for your confidence and understanding."[66]

On April 27 Flood went to New York's Kennedy Airport and boarded a plane bound for Barcelona. He disembarked during a layover in Lisbon, and rerouted himself to Copenhagen, where he had spent the previous summer.

Though he attempted to disguise his troubles, the weighty burden he carried was noticeable to most who crossed his path. " Obviously he has some deep personal problems that I knew little about," Marvin Miller said to a reporter. "I talked on the phone with Curt last week when the Senators were in New York. He said he was fine. He always said that."[67]

"I don't think we'll ever see him back in this country," a member of Washington's front office remarked. "Troubles like he has just don't go away."[68]

As could be expected, the game's commentators lined up in opposition to Flood's legal stance. The vast majority of baseball scribes viewed the lawsuit as a traitorous undertaking and none were more vocal than Dick Young, whose prose could be found in the pages of *The Sporting News.*

"He (Flood) was not the best possible example for the Player's Association to use in its attack on the contentious reserve clause," Young wrote. "He was a high priced star, on the way down, obviously overpaid, hardly one to convey the 'slave image,' which his counsel strove to depict. The one thing he had going for him: he is Black and therefore the sentimental favorite of the time."[69]

If the owners had wanted a mouthpiece in the press, Young certainly fit the bill. Of the scant few writers who defended Flood, Leonard Koppett of *The New York Times* was the most outspoken. Koppett well understood the human side of Curt's plight, and recognized an individual's right to economic freedom. Young and his ilk tended to view the lawsuit in terms of greed: Flood's and the Player's Association's. Koppett's voice was rare

Curt Flood during his brief start with the Washington Senators (author's collection).

in a melieu bloated with newsmen of the old guard. Change, especially change instigated by a Black man, offended the senses of the men who chronicled the game.

The tribulations of the preceding year and a half, and the repetitious diatribes against his character (and skin color) left their mark on Curt. Any faith Flood may have had in the media's objectivity had vanished. For over a year, Curt was subjected to daily doses of newsprint that demonized him as the great destroyer of the nation's grand game.

He retreated from his country and the world of baseball. Curt fled America and her broken promises to salve his wounds.

Baby, I Gave Them One Hell of a Fight

> Power is not the white man's birthright; it will not be legislated for us and delivered in neat government packages. It is a social force any group can utilize by accumulating its elements in a planned, deliberate campaign to organize it under its own control.[70]
>
> Martin Luther King, Jr., "Black Power Defined"

The Supreme Court heard oral arguments in *Flood v Kuhn* on March 20, 1972. Three months later, the Court rendered a 5-3 verdict in favor of the defendant, with Justice Powell abstaining.

Justice Blackmun wrote the majority decision, which began with an embarrassing paean to the National Pastime.

"Ty Cobb, Babe Ruth, Walter Johnson, Henry Chadwick..." the litany of baseball icons continued ad nauseam until eighty-eight past greats were conjured. Astoundingly, none of the players named in Blackmun's original draft were African American. Justice Thurgood Marshall, upon reading this circulated version, contacted Blackmun and criticized such a blatant omission

"But there were no Black players during the golden age of baseball," Blackmun told Marshall.

"Precisely my point,"[71] Marshall replied. Reluctantly, Blackmun added the names of Jackie Robinson, Satchel Paige, and Roy Campenella to the published text.

Baseball's antitrust exemption was, according to the opinion, "an aberration that has been with us now for half a century, one heretofore deemed fully entitled to the benefit of stare decisis, and one that has survived the Court's expanding concept of interstate commerce. It rests on a recognition and acceptance of baseball's unique characteristics."[72]

Blackmun all but admitted in his opinion that the game's exemption was an anomaly. Still, the Justice and his conservative brethren on the bench refused to overturn a previous Court's ruling.

The liberals on the Court, led by Thurgood Marshall, weren't swayed by the game's mythology. While Blackmun cited "Casey at the Bat," and "Tinker to Evers to Chance," Marshall examined America's infatuation with professional athletes.

"Americans love baseball as they love all sports," Marshall wrote in the dissenting opinion. "Perhaps we become so enamored of athletes that we assume that they are foremost in the minds of legislatures as well as fans. We must not forget, however, that there are only some 600 major league baseball players. Whatever muscle they might have been able to muster by combining forces with other athletes has been greatly impaired by the manner in which this court has isolated them. It is this court that has made them impotent, and this court should correct its error.

"To non-athletes, it might appear that petitioner was virtually enslaved by the owners of major league baseball clubs who bartered among themselves for his services. But, athletes know that it was not servitude that bound petitioner to the club owners; it was the reserve system."[73]

A crestfallen but unwavering Flood descended the steps of the Supreme Courts building after the verdict was read "Baby, I gave them one hell of a fight,"[74] he told gathered newsmen.

Flood's courageous action may have resulted in a personal defeat; however, his direct attack upon the reserve system laid bare its vulnerability. Despite the High Court's ruling, Marvin Miller firmly believed that progress had been made on behalf of all players. "The climate now is much more favorable for meaningful negotiations,"[75] Miller said.

It is fitting that a Black man stepped forward and struck the first blow in the players struggle for fiscal freedom. To some, the reserve system was analogous to indentured servitude. Flood's dispute with baseball found its rightful place in a tumultuous era. Curt's fight came to pass in the shadows of a multitude of significant cultural events. Black leaders-— Medgar Evers, Malcolm X, Martin Luther King Jr.-— were martyred by assassins' bullets. Riots raged in the streets of American cities. The world's heavyweight champion was stripped of his title in the aftermath of his refusal to fight in a racist war.

In his own revolutionary manner, Curt Flood sought to right his own "corner of society."[76] His argument was steeped in the tradition of personal freedom ... a fulfillment of values long espoused by champions of democracy.

"I was offended by the disparity between American reality and American pretension," Flood wrote. "I wanted reality upgraded, pretension abolished… The hypocrisies of the baseball industry could not possibly have been sustained unless they were symptoms of a wider affliction. Wherever I turned, I found fresh evidence that this was so. Baseball was socially relevant, and so was my rebellion against it."[77]

Though defeated in the land's highest court, Flood's legacy would cast a long shadow on the game. Flood would never financially benefit from his strife. Instead, he was lampooned and belittled, verbally crucified by his detractors, his motivations consistently misrepresented.

"I'm pleased that God made my skin Black," Curt acknowledged. "I just wish he had made it thicker."[78]

5

David the Star: *Dave Parker*

He walked onto the field, barely recognizable. The great athlete was now a shadow of his former self: his hair snowy white, his step slowed to a shuffling gait, his eyesight all but gone. Physical ailments may have slowed the regal pioneer, yet the righteous indignation remained untouched by the gathering of time.

On October 15, 1972, baseball honored Jackie Robinson and the twenty-fifth anniversary of the game's integration. The fifty-three-year-old Robinson was asked to throw out the first ball at Game Two of the World Series which pitted the Oakland A's against the Cincinnati Reds.

Moments before throwing out the honorary pitch, Robinson addressed a national television audience. "I am extremely proud and pleased," he said, " but I'm going to be tremendously more pleased and more proud when I look at that third base coaching line one day and see a Black face managing the ball club."[1]

Jackie Robinson died nine days later, his resolve and conviction intact.

Robinson's hopeful optimism was tempered by reality; baseball remained lethargic in its updating hiring practices. Gene Baker became the first Black to manage in organized ball when the Pittsburgh Pirates hired him to manage their Batavia affiliate prior to the 1961 season. Baker was an anomaly, however, as managerial positions throughout professional baseball continued to be a lily-white bastion. A Black candidate for a managerial opening would have to have *special* qualities, a requirement even the more liberal in the baseball community admitted.

"A man will have to have more stability to be a Negro coach or a manager and be slower to anger than if he were white," Bill Veeck estimated in 1960. "The first major league manager will have to be a fellow who has

Jackie Robinson throwing out the first pitch at Game Two of the 1972 World Series (© Bettmann/CORBIS).

been playing extremely well for a dozen years or so, so that he becomes a byword for excellence."[2]

These special qualifications were little more than a pretext to justify the old-boy network that governed the game's hierarchy. When the managerial barrier was finally crossed, Veeck's prophecy was proven to be true. In 1975, the Cleveland Indians hired future Hall of Famer Frank Robinson to be a player/manager. Three years later Larry Doby would become the majors' second Black manager when Bill Veeck hired him to take the helm of his Chicago White Sox.

Thirteen months prior to Jackie Robinson's challenge for the game to correct its inequitable hiring practices, a major league club, for the first and only time, fielded an all-Black lineup. Fittingly, the occasion took place in Pittsburgh, home to a glorious history of Black baseball.

On September 1, 1971, the Pirates fulfilled the value inherent in the game, and indeed in America herself: "*the best man plays.*"

"I was always proud of the fact that we never paid any attention to color in our organization," Pirates general manager Joe Brown said. "Nine Blacks in the lineup at one time I think epitomized what our organizational policy was: 'the best man plays,' 'the best man makes the Pittsburgh club.'"[3]

For more than a decade, Pittsburgh exemplified the democratic ideal set in motion by Jackie Robinson's heroic venture. Pirate ball clubs of the late sixties and early seventies consistently had from 10 to 13 minority players on its roster. The Pirates' first-rate scouting department scoured urban America, Latin America, and the Caribbean in search of quality ball players. Joe Brown's color-blind philosophy not only culminated in a World Championship in 1971, it fostered a spirit of well-muscled confidence, an attribute that became the signature of not only the Pittsburgh teams, but a new generation of Black athletes.

> It's a competitive thing to live in a ghetto. You're always thinking, "I'm going to get out some way."[4]
>
> Dave Parker

Dave Parker's intimidating stature was softened by his warm and engaging smile. The immense Parker was a striking presence; his towering physicality looming over his contemporaries. Complementing his God-given attributes was a gift for panache. Parker's stylish bearing brought notice and induced commentary.

In addition to the diamond stud in his left earlobe, Dave accessorized with a conspicuous Star of David worn on a gold chain around his neck. An elderly Jewish woman whom Dave had met while playing winter ball in Venezuela gave him the Star of David. "Wear this, it will take care of you," she told Parker.

Such an explanation, perfectly suitable though it may be, lacked a certain flamboyance. When asked about the piece of jewelry Parker shortened the tale down to its bare essentials.

"It gets tiring going through the whole story about how I got the star," he explained, "so when people ask why I wear it I just say, 'Well, I'm David and I'm a Star.' They usually buy it, too. After all, it's true isn't it?"[5]

Dave Parker was born in Calhoun, Mississippi, on June 9, 1951. Richard Parker relocated his family to Cincinnati, Ohio, when Dave was four years old. "I saw my father struggle through life," Dave said. "He supported six kids with a job that didn't pay much money, yet it was a happy household. He found time for humor even though he didn't reap the benefit of his job.

"I came from a pretty rough environment. I lived in a hard neighborhood and sports was a means of getting out. That was brought to my attention as soon as they found out I had some ability in baseball."[6]

Parker lived two blocks from Crosley Field, the home of Cincinnati's Reds. As a youngster Dave would often hang around outside the park in hopes of seeing his heroes, Frank Robinson and Vada Pinson. Eventually he made it inside the ball yard by getting a job as a vendor in the park. He brought home little pay, though, as Dave spent more time as a spectator than as a salesman.

"I was the worst hot dog vendor in history," Parker remembered. "I just watched Frank and Vada, never sold any hot dogs. I'd go home and fantasize about being them, having cars like they did, matching white Thunderbirds with red upholstery ... I told my mother that I was going to grow up and buy her a house."[7]

For a time, through, it seemed as if Dave's route out of the Cincinnati ghetto would be football. As a running back at Courter Tech, Parker caught the attention of numerous college scouts. In the aftermath of a brilliant junior season in which he gained 1,365 yards, Dave received scholarship offers from practically every big name school. All hopes of playing major college football, however, were dashed early in Dave's senior year.

"I ripped a cartilage on an end sweep, and I had to have it removed from my left knee,"[8] Parker explained. The injury brought Dave's football career to a sudden halt. Virtually all of the sixty-two scholarship offers he had received were summarily revoked. Ohio State and Michigan were among the universities that wanted no part of a running back with a highly questionable knee.

Dave's injury not only cost him a chance at a Division I football scholarship; it also had a dramatic effect on his standing in the annual baseball draft. The Pittsburgh Pirates selected Parker in the 14th round of the 1970 June free-agent draft. "The Reds had been watching him all along," Pittsburgh scout Howie Haak reported. "They laughed at us when we took him."[9]

"I signed for $6,500." Dave said. "If it wasn't for my bad knee, I would have been picked in the first or second round. It cost me about $90,000 or $95,000."[10]

Parker proved very early in his professional career that his knee was sound, batting .317 as a member of the Bradenton Pirates in the Rookie League. Parker's star rose quickly in the Pittsburgh organization. Following the premature death of Roberto Clemente in an airplane crash December 31, 1972, all eyes focused on the Pirate farmhand as the savior of the organization.

"I know a lot of people talk about me being another Clemente or another Stargell, but I wish they wouldn't," Dave said in 1973 while stationed in Charleston, West Virginia. "I just want to be known as the first Dave Parker."[11]

Dave received his promotion to the major leagues on July 11, 1973. "I was in Charleston washing dishes, and I found out that I had a two o'clock flight leaving from Chicago, and a direct flight to San Diego," Parker said. "I was so nervous that I packed in about three minutes. I left the dishwater in the sink, and combed my hair on the way downstairs while dragging my luggage."

On the plane, en route to catch up with the Pirates on the west coast, Dave tried to soothe his nerves. "I had about three Bloody Marys," he remembered. "So I was half-tanked before I got there."[12]"

Parker arrived at Jack Murphy Stadium in the 7th inning but was not used in the contest. Pittsburgh manager Bill Virdon opted not to place Dave in the lineup until the following day. "The next day I started ... first four at-bats—all line drives. Didn't get one hit." Dave began his career 0–10."[13]

> Pittsburgh traditionally has the loudest, trashiest-mouthed, loosest, most uproarious dressing room in baseball. People are forever doing unflattering imitations of each other, lifting each other up bodily, defaming each other's heritages and threatening each other's lives.[14]
>
> Roy Blount, Jr.

Joe Brown had a custom of asking his players to make new additions to feel at home.

"I idolized Clemente in some ways," Parker relayed. "In spring training of '71 I worked out with him in the outfield. He would say, 'Woo, I used to be able to throw like that.' I found that to be a relaxing thing.

"And Stargell took me under his wing. He is a soft-spoken, very kind individual, 24-karat gold.

"The first time I saw Dock Ellis, here he comes in white pants with a purple stripe down the side, a purple suede jacket with spangles hanging and a little band around his head. He was wearing about four rings."[15]

Confidence and certainty oozed throughout the Pirate clubhouse. "There was some cockiness in us," Pirate center-fielder Al Oliver admitted, "but it was a good cockiness. It showed in the way we played the game. It was an attitude. 'The Battlin' Bucs' moniker fit us perfectly.

"If an opposing pitcher had eavesdropped on us rapping in the locker room prior to a game, they wouldn't have taken the mound. We may have talked a better game than we played. To hear us tell it, we were each going to get five hits in that evening's game."[16]

Don Sutton, pitcher for the Los Angeles Dodgers, humorously analyzed Pittsburgh hitters. "Each club has a special hitting personality," Sutton said. "One club will watch your delivery and say, 'Oh boy, here comes a fastball.' And they'll jump on it. Others say, 'Oh boy, here's a changeup.' The Pirates just say, 'Oh boy, here comes a baseball.'"[17]

Parker immediately felt at home in the Pirates' swaggering clubhouse. Dave could talk smack with the best, but more importantly, he would follow through on his boasts.

"I don't think I felt any pressure," Dave said. "Roberto was a great superstar. I didn't think I could go out there and give that up-tempo type of performance that he did for so many years. I knew there wasn't any way that I could go out and flash like Clemente. But I knew that I had some things of my own. Now that I've learned how to play the position, my ability will run neck and neck with his."[18]

There's a Riot Goin' On

The first strike in professional sports began on March 31, 1972. On the surface, the dispute that forced the strike was relatively minor. The Player's Association was seeking a cost of living increase in welfare and pension benefits; the owners did not want to ante up any additional cash despite enjoying a large infusion of television money since the prior contract settlement in 1969.

For management, the confrontation wasn't centered on capital. Instead, their concern was the preservation of power. The owners' goal in 1972 was to break the will of the players, and in doing so sap the strength of the Player's Association. Any chance of the owners reaching their goal was quashed before the strike even began, thanks to Gussie Busch's defiant challenge to the union.

"We're not going to give them another goddamn cent," the Cardinals owner said to members of the press. "We voted unanimously to take a stand. If they want to strike let them strike."

Gussie's words rang in the ears of the rank and file. Instead of shaking the player's resolve, Busch's statement became a rallying point, according to Marvin Miller.[19]

The players didn't crack. Thirteen days into the walkout, management capitulated. Had ownership not taken such an ill-advised stance, the impasse could easily have been avoided. The two sides agreed to the proposal put forth by the Player's Association prior to the strike.

In the pages of the *New York Times*, Leonard Koppet summarized the dispute.

> PLAYERS: We want higher pensions
> OWNERS: We won't give you one damn cent.
> PLAYERS: You don't have to—the money is already there. Just let us use it.
> OWNERS: It would be imprudent.

PLAYERS: We did it before and anyhow, we won't play unless we can have some of it.
OWNERS: Okay.[20]

The '72 strike would be remembered not for increased pension funds, but for the collapse of the owners' autocratic rule. Their innocence gone, the players discovered what solidarity in the ranks could accomplish.

The National Pastime would never be the same.

Though it was little noted at the time, Marvin Miller had made a large stride toward economic equality for major-league baseball players when he pushed for, and received, an independent arbitrator in the 1970 Basic Agreement. In time, it would be an arbitrator by the name of Peter Seitz who would "set the players free."

One specific line in paragraph 10 (a) of the Uniform Player's Contract drew the attention of Marvin Miller. The owners had a right to renew an unsigned player *for one year only.* "With impartial arbitration in effect, we could argue the meaning and interpretation of a contract provision," Miller reasoned. "It was only a matter of time, I felt, before we could test whether a club's right of renewal of a contract lasted forever or existed for one additional year.

"We need the language of the contract to mean what it says. If you're not in agreement on salary by March 1, the club can, in the next ten days, renew your contract for one year. That means you're under contract again and not required to sign anything. By signing last year's contract, you've given the club the option to unilaterally renew.

"In my view, the contract is clear. At the end of that season, there's no further contractual tie between the player and his club. He can become a free agent."[21]

In 1969, Al Downing of the New York Yankees attempted to play without a newly signed contract. Downing's attempt to play without a contract was quickly repudiated by Yankee G.M. Lee MacPahil. The pitcher was told that he couldn't play without a new agreement, but Downing pointed out to MacPahil that when he signed his contract the previous season the Yankees automatically held an option for the next.

Had New York forced Downing to leave training camp, the player would have become a free agent due to the club's violation of the contract. MacPahil wasn't willing to risk allowing Downing to play out the season without a new contract. Nor was he willing to set Al loose as a free agent. Instead, Downing was offered a small raise for the 1969 season, which he readily accepted.

Over the course of the next five years, similar scenarios were played out. Ted Simmons, Sparky Lyle, and Bobby Tolan, among others, all played without a contract for various reasons and varying lengths of time. Similarly, each man reached an agreement before Paragraph 10 (a) could be challenged before an arbitrator. Still, Miller was encouraged: The owners were panic-stricken by the thought of a player bringing the Association's argument to an arbitrator.

Finally, following the 1975 season, Miller had a test case by the name of Andy Messersmith. Messersmith asked that the Los Angeles Dodgers insert a "no-trade" clause in any contract that he would sign. Prior to Messersmith's demand, such an amendment was unheard of in the history of the game. "I'm going to have some control of my destiny," Messersmith told reporters.

Los Angeles owner Peter O'Malley resolutely refused to acquiesce to his pitcher's stipulation. "We've never given one [a no-trade clause] and we aren't going to start now,"[22] O'Malley declared.

In case Messersmith caved in and signed with the Dodgers at the last minute, Miller found an insurance policy for his test case in Dave McNally, a recently retired pitcher.

McNally had been traded from the Baltimore Orioles to the Montreal Expos following the '74 season, and refused to sign a new contract with his new club. Upset with the trade and unhappy in his new surroundings, McNally quit the Expos after a June 8 doubleheader. Miller contacted McNally, hoping to entice the pitcher into lending his name to any possible arbitration.

"Are you coming back to play?" Miller asked McNally.

"No, never," McNally replied.

"I'd like to add your name to the grievance as insurance if Andy decides to sign a new Dodger contract."

"If you need me, I'm willing to help," McNally assured Miller.

Within several days, Montreal general manager John McHale contacted the pitcher. The Expos wanted him back, so much so that McHale offered Dave the astounding sum of $125,000 to sign for the 1976 season.

"Gee I don't know," McNally to the G.M. "I'm not sure I can ever pitch at the major league level anymore."

"Don't worry about it," McHale assured him. "I'll give you $25,000 just to sign and come to spring training."

McNally held his ground. "It's tempting to show up in spring training for twenty-five grand," he admitted to Miller, "but I have no intention of playing, and it wouldn't be right to take the money."[23]

To Miller's relief Messersmith did not sign and McNally was able to resist the temptation of Montreal's disproportionate offer. In early October, the union filed grievances in the pitchers' names. Arbitrating the case would be Peter Seitz, who one year earlier had freed Jim "Catfish" Hunter from his contract with the Oakland A's. Hunter had filed a grievance against Athletics owner Charley Finley for breach of contract. Following Seitz's decision, Hunter became baseball's first free agent and agreed to an enormous new contract with the New York Yankees.

After hearing the arguments from both sides in the Messersmith/McNally case, Seitz pleaded with Miller and management's attorney, John Gaherin, to negotiate a settlement. "Look, take this case out of my hands," Seitz begged. "Negotiate with the players and settle your differences."

Gaherin took Seitz's request back to the owners. "If you read this the way I do here's what Seitz is saying: 'Let this chalice pass from me, Father, but if I have to drink it I'm going to spit it all over you.'"[24]

The owners refused to heed Gaherin's advice. "You want to give away this industry," Gussie Busch charged. "Bullshit! Bullshit!"[25]

Gaherin reluctantly picked up a phone and called Miller. "There's no change in our position," Gaherin told Miller. "The clubs feel they have a vested right in the player."[26]

The decision was then placed in the lap of Seitz, who, two weeks later, declared his ruling. "The grievances of Messersmith and McNally are sustained. There is no contractual bond between these players and the Los Angeles and the Montreal clubs, respectively." [27]"

Immediately upon placing his signature on the "Dissent" line of the ruling, Gaherin handed Seitz a letter informing him that he had been fired as baseball's arbitrator.

Baseball's owners were a far from enlightened group. Messersmith was an aberration, they believed: the reserve clause remained alive and well. The lords of the game immediately filed suit in federal court, hoping to overturn Seitz's decision. After *Messersmith* was upheld in Kansas City district court, the owners took their case to circuit court. Again, Seitz was upheld.

For nearly a century the court system had repeatedly come to the aid of baseball's ruling class; suddenly they were backed into a corner and forced to negotiate with the Player's Association.

The Basic Agreement signed in 1972 expired on December 31, 1975, and management "were offering us ice in the winter,"[28] according to Marvin Miller.

"I figured that management would take the offensive," Miller wrote in his memoirs. "In other words: a lockout. The lockout, of course, was management's way of testing their misguided theory that the players would be unable to remain united."[29]

It was management, though, who failed to stay united. An eighteen-day lockout ended when Commissioner Kuhn opened the spring camps, an action that infuriated his bosses. "What? But we've got 'em!"[30] an incredulous Calvin Griffith said when he heard of Kuhn's move.

"Whatever shred of credibility we had for being able to engage in hardball negotiations [is] gone,"[31] moaned Player Relations Committee lawyer Barry Rona.

At the start of spring training, more than 350 players were unsigned, and would be eligible for free agency following the '76 season. Miller did not want to flood the market with players each season; the simple equation of supply and demand would not allow entitled players to receive an optimum contract.

Miller agonized over a fair service requirement for players to become eligible for free agency. Ownership proposed a ten-year service requirement, which the Player's Association rejected out of hand. The average career for a major league player was well short of ten years, and those men who played for more than a decade had, more often than not, seen their prime earning years pass.

Miller counter-proposed that players with four years of service would be eligible. "My feeling," Miller explained, "was that five years would be better and that if the choice lay between four and six years, I would choose the latter."[32]

Months of debate culminated on July 12, the eve of baseball's All-Star break. The Player's Association agreed to a six-year service requirement for free agency, with additional concessions by the owners: the player with five years' service had a right to demand a trade; the player could designate up to six teams to which he would not accept a trade, and, should his club fail to trade him by March 15 said player would have the right to become a free agent.

Nearly a century of tyrannical control had been significantly weakened. The owners' stranglehold on their subjects—the reserve clause—had been considerably loosened.

I Believe in Myself

Sports Illustrated asked in its April 9, 1979, edition, "Who's the Best?" Gracing the cover of the national sports weekly were the 1978 National and American League MVPs, Dave Parker and Jim Rice, respectively.

Rice, a veteran of five years, was coming off a brilliant season that saw him bat .315, drive in 139 runs and belt 46 home runs. The Boston Red Sox left fielder posed back-to-back with Parker; his arms crossed, sporting a bemused smile upon his face, glancing askance at his contemporary from Pittsburgh.

For his part, Parker knew the answer to the query posed by the magazine. With a broad grin spread across his handsome face, Dave gazed knowingly into the camera's lens all the while holding aloft the index finger of his right hand.

"I am the best talent in baseball today," Dave reported. "I'm going to get 3,000 hits. I'm going to set the record for most hits in a game. This year, when the leaves turn brown, I'll have the Triple Crown. I'm probably going to bat .400 one day. It may sound unreal, but I think in terms of dreams that are dreamt to be lived."[33]

Parker's brazen honesty did not set well with either the sporting press or the fans of the game. However inflated his ego, though, Dave was correct in his appraisal: "I believe in myself."[34]

Dave Parker was of the Ali generation: "I am the greatest." Ali's proclamation became part of the American lexicon, and the passion invoked by his declaration was passed on to the generation that followed his rise to fame. Perhaps more than any of his contemporaries, Dave Parker embodied this spirit.

"The great Ali says the reason he talks a lot is that he puts himself on the line and then has to go out and back it up," Parker said. "I push myself in that regard."[35]

Parker's mode of self-motivation was quite effective. No player was Dave's equal during the latter half of the 1970s. Parker combined fine foot speed with a batting stroke that delivered a high average and respectable power numbers. As a right fielder, he was the finest in the game.

"There's only one thing bigger than me," Dave told reporters, "and that's my ego."

"The greatest ever? With my attitude I can't see anything but that. I think I have the potential to be the greatest ever to have played."[36]

Through six seasons Dave lived up to and reached his potential. His offensive numbers read:

851 hits
97 HR's
439 RBI's
410 RUNS
68 stolen bases
.318 average.

These added up to two batting titles, and for the 1978 season a Most Valuable Player award.

Parker's finest season culminated in a landslide vote of the Baseball

Writer's Association of America, garnering 21 of 24 first-place votes. Parker's accomplishments came during a season in which he fractured his cheekbone in a play at the plate. Dave missed 11 games due to the injury and played the final thirteen weeks wearing a football facemask attached to his batting helmet.

"Two things for sure, the sun's gonna shine, and I'm going three for four,"[37] Parker was heard to say.

"Why do Black people tend to shout?" essayist Ralph Riley rhetorically asked. "Black people tend to shout in churches, movie theaters, and anywhere else they feel the need to shout, because when joy, pain, anger, confusion and frustration, ego and thought, mix it up, the way they do inside Black people, the uproar is too big to hold inside. The feeling must be aired."[38]

In the post–*Messersmith* world of baseball, timing was nearly as important as ability, and Dave's timing was impeccable. 1979 would be Parker's option year, making him eligible for free agency following that season. As a small-market team, Pittsburgh would have no chance of retaining Parker's services should Dave test the free-agent market.

Following the 1977 season, a year in which Dave captured his first batting title, Parker began campaigning for a renegotiated contract. "Rene-

Dave Parker: "Two things for sure: the sun's gonna shine, and I'm going three for four" (© Bettmann/CORBIS).

gotiate is the wrong word," Dick Moss, legal counsel for the Player's Association explained. "In these situations the player isn't asking to renegotiate, he's asking for a new contract to extend beyond the life of the current contract. And certainly it would be to the club's advantage to have a player of Parker's value signed to a longer contract. It would be just as beneficial to the club as to the player."[39]

At $200,000 per season, Parker believed that he was vastly underpaid. "I feel I'm one of the best talents in baseball and I want to be paid like one of the best," Dave said. "I hope we can come to some kind of contract. I'd like to stay in Pittsburgh. I love the personnel and the city."[40]

Parker had little leverage other than his outstanding talent and a penchant for speaking his mind to the press. "How would I look in a Philadelphia uniform?" he would ask writers. "I'd like to come back to Pittsburgh and tear the stadium down with base hits. .[41]"

The verbal barrage from the right fielder continued, as did the base hits. With every home run and run batted in, Parker's bargaining position strengthened.

"A lot of guys have been unhappy with management," Dave told *Black Sports Magazine.* "I think it's the club's responsibility to keep its players, you know, happy. There's been something of a problem in that area here."[42]

The impasse was broken after Pete Rose signed with the Philadelphia Phillies as a free agent. The Pirates were one of many clubs vying for the services of Rose, and their missing out on the opportunity to sign the fiery player indirectly affected Parker's status. Rose strengthened a club that was already Pittsburgh's toughest division foe. In light of Rose's new-found fortune, the necessity to retain Parker's services for the long term was greatly enhanced. The Rose inking set a benchmark for Dave's value on the open market. At 38 years old Rose was a fraction of the player Parker was at 27. For Dave, negotiations would *begin* at the $3.4 million garnered by Rose.

Nearly two years of posturing in the media came to a climax on Friday January 26, 1979, when Parker became the highest-paid player in baseball. The agreement would earn Dave $4.5 million over the life of the five-year contract.

"I'm very content," Parker said. "This contract will keep me in Pittsburgh the rest of my playing career. This is where I want to play. The ball club is my family."

We Are Fam-i-lee

Nineteen seventy-nine was to be a magical year for the Pittsburgh Pirates. The Pirates' enchanted season culminated in a victory against the

Baltimore Orioles in Game Seven of the World Series. Dave Parker continued to sparkle on the field, as evidenced by his MVP performance in the mid summer classic. However, the glory of the '79 season was tainted for Parker. The only credentials that mattered to a growing segment of the fans who ventured to Three Rivers were the numbers on Parker's contract; the batting titles, Gold Gloves and MVPs were immaterial.

> With all your fortune and fame, you're a stinkin' Nigger just the same.[43]
>
> Anonymous letter to Parker

Dave had fulfilled his dream and ambition of winning a championship with his mentor, Willie Stargell. The hype and notoriety that surrounded the "We are Family" aspect of that championship club somewhat diminished the authentic affection members of the team felt for each other. Starting at the top, with manager Chuck Tanner's effusive enthusiasm and heartfelt backslapping, the club's "team" mentality filtered throughout the locker room.

"The 'Family' thing was genuine, and it was great," Parker said upon reflection. "But I still get the feeling that somebody out there didn't like me. You do tend to get that feeling when your own fans start throwing batteries at your back while you're playing in the outfield."[44]

The World Championship season, as fulfilling as it was, remained a bittersweet time for Parker. The relationship between Dave and Pittsburgh fans had grown increasingly antagonistic over the course of the year. Parker's rapport with the fans had become so strained that he did not bother to attend the victory parade in downtown Pittsburgh following the Series victory.

"Why should I?" he asked. "Why just last season some people were throwing garbage at me."[45]

Like the seventh inning stretch and the playing of "The Star Spangled Banner," taunts and heckles delivered by the paying customers belong to the game. For generations fans have jeered and mocked players from visiting teams, or perhaps a hometown hero mired in a slump. Boos and catcalls are a traditional staple in a sport immersed in tradition. In Pittsburgh, however, the right-field faithful occasionally crossed the line between one's God given right to voice displeasure at the ol' ball yard, and offensive speech.

"There are a lot of sick people in the world and I know most of them don't live in Pittsburgh, but sometimes it seems that way," Parker said. "I'm like a guy without a hometown. I'm on the road all the time. If the fans pay their $5.50 and $6.50, they're entitled to voice their opinion. But when they break the windows in Willie Stargell's Rolls-Royce or slash the roof of my car, that infuriates."[46]

The verbal taunts were accompanied by an occasional missile heaved from the stands towards Parker's position in right field. The "tradition" of bombarding Parker with various objects, which was initiated in the summer of '79, continued throughout the rest of Dave's Pirate career.

On July 19, 1980, during the eighth inning of the first game of a doubleheader against the Dodgers, a transistor battery was thrown at Parker. Dave picked the object up and walked off the field, not to return for the remainder of the afternoon.

"I was hit in the back of the head with a gas valve from a pellet gun last year," he said following the game. "Sunday it was a battery. Earlier this year somebody tossed a sock full of nuts and bolts that weighed five pounds."[47]

"I saw the whole disgusting thing," teammate Kent Tekulve said. "They threw nuts and bolts and bullets and batteries at him. On bat day, I saw a father take his kid's bat away and throw it at Parker. He tried to hurt him, and he cost his kid a bat. Those fans thought they were seeing a giant man who didn't care about anybody but Dave Parker. They were dead wrong ... he was as valuable off the field as he was on."[48]

Why Pirate fans turned on Parker so abruptly and completely is open to speculation. Race and economic conditions in the Steel City certainly played their roles in the emotional, and sometimes violent, reaction to Parker.

"Pittsburgh's basically a blue-collar town," Dave said. "They think people making all that money ought to work hard for it and they don't think a baseball player does. It's been proven that they don't come to games because, they say, 'There are too many Blacks and Puerto Ricans playing.'

"I hate to think of it that way, but evidently it is. I'd like to think this club reflects the city ... hard working and dedicated. I hope we can forget who's on the field and what color he is."[49]

Parker was not the first to express the suspicion that Pittsburgh fans were avoiding Three Rivers because of the great number of minorities on the Pirates. These thoughts had long been whispered throughout the city, and the question was raised in 1975 when Dock Ellis told the *Pittsburgh Post-Gazette*'s Charley Feeney that people were staying away from games because there were "too many Blacks."[50] Ellis's charge couldn't possibly be proven; however, attendance at Pirates contests throughout the seventies certainly didn't correlate with the success rate of the ball club.

The issue again was brought to the fore in 1982 when Howie Haak told a Pittsburgh writer that fans were avoiding Pirate games because of the preponderance of Blacks on the team. Shortly after Haak's comments made headlines in the city's papers, the Pirates traded Eddie Solomon to the White Sox for Jim Morrison and Bill Robinson to the Phillies in exchange for Wayne Nordhagen.

"Did you check the attendance?" Parker shouted out in the Buc clubhouse the evening after the trade. "They had more tonight than they did last night. They trade two (Blacks) and get two whites and that's what happens. If they ever trade me, they'll fill up the stadium."

"Hey Howie," Dave shouted to the Pirate scout. "See what happens when you shoot off your mouth to the papers.... Two brothers go down the tubes."[51]

Even though a number of Pirates joked about the coincidence of the transaction in the aftermath of Haak's interview, only Parker's remarks were reported in the press. Parker's delivery was, more often than not, accompanied by a beaming smile. His lighthearted intent was not expressed in print. Rather, the sports reporters in Pittsburgh enjoyed portraying Parker as a boorish louse. Dave's on-field exploits were continually downplayed and the media painted an evolving portrait of Parker a villainous, egocentric loudmouth.

"Fans were down on me, but I blame much of that on the media," Dave said. "Rarely was anything positive written or said about me. I never tried to abuse anyone, yet I was the clubhouse bully. Sure, I'm loud, but I'm a positive guy and I said a lot that I didn't intend to show up in the papers. I tried to help people, but Dave Parker was a grossly misunderstood man.

"For a two-week stretch, 14 days, there was a story on me every day in the Pittsburgh newspapers. And every one of them was negative. I had injuries, but I did the best I could."[52]

Writers picked at every aspect of Parker's being, including his choice of jewelry. In a *Sport* magazine interview journalist Jim O'Brien chastised Parker for the earring that Dave sported in his left ear, a rare sight in the seventies. "You'd be better off if you didn't wear it," O'Brien lectured. "To the fans it doesn't signify strength. It suggests something queer in their mind."[53]

"I think I reflect everything in the field that a ballplayer is supposed to reflect," Dave answered, " but I'm positive and outspoken and I don't think I should be persecuted for that. So, if the city can't accept me, I think it's a good time to move on."[54]

By 1982, Parker was the most despised man in Pittsburgh sports. The ill feeling that began in '79, snowballed as Dave's production started to falter beginning with the 1981 season. A key contribution to Parker's dwindling potency on the field was a spate of injuries that would plague him for the remainder of his Pirates career.

In 1981, Dave tried to check his swing on a pitch delivered by Nolan Ryan and ruptured ligaments in his right wrist. Later in the same contest, with Ryan still on the mound, Parker again tried to check his swing, this time incurring ligament damage in his left wrist. The wrist was placed in a cast for a month.

During a 1982 contest against the Phillies, Dave jammed his thumb sliding into second base while trying to stretch a single into a double. "That injury knocked me out for six weeks," Parker said. "And I had an Achilles tendon problem all though the 1983 season."[55]

Pittsburgh fans, as would be expected, were unsympathetic to Dave's tribulations. What they saw was an overweight, underachieving (*Black*) multi-millionaire.

"The steel industry was bad and the coal industry was bad and people couldn't relate to a multi-millionaire ball player. Their attitude totally changed toward me," Parker explained.

"If I went out in Pittsburgh during that time, I would have been confronted and I didn't run away from no challenge. So to avoid popping somebody in the head and me being sued, I turned into a hermit. I seldom left my house. If I had been a white guy at the time I had received the money, they would have erected a shrine to me in that city for all I did."[56]

Pittsburgh may have been the first, but they certainly weren't the only city to lash out at Parker.

At Philadelphia's Veterans Stadium, two .38 caliber bullets were thrown at Parker.

In Dave's hometown of Cincinnati, he was pelted with apple cores and empty beer cups.

The projectile of choice in Montreal was a variety of fruit. "They threw oranges at me and hit me in the leg with an apple," Dave reported. "It's gotten to the point where I consider it a good day to come away from the park alive."[57]

"Early in my career I couldn't wait to go to the ballpark," Dave said. "I used to arrive at 2:30, like five hours before the start of a night game. But after baseball stopped being fun, I'd make it a point not to get to the park until 5:30, not until I absolutely had to get there."[58]

Dave spent the summer of '83 biding his time. His contract with Pittsburgh would be up at the close of the season, and there was no doubt that Dave would not be returning to the Steel City. The deterioration of Dave's relationship with Pirates fans had eroded beyond any hope of repair. The *coup-de-grace* came late in the '83 season when Parker was warming up in the outfield at Three Rivers and an object landed on the turf just a few feet away from him. Parker sauntered over, scooped up the missile, which turned out to be a radio battery, and gave it to the first-base umpire before returning to his position.

The incident embodied the animus between the player and the fans. A significant portion of Pirate fans would gladly have ridden Parker out of town on a rail; Dave, despite having his work place converted into a war zone, never blinked.

"I have 19, 20, more days on my contract and no one is going to intimidate me out of there,"[59] he defiantly said following the latest attack.

A Modern-Day Lynching

For two weeks in September 1985, the eyes of the baseball world were focused on Pittsburgh. Unfortunately for the welfare of the game, those eyes were not concentrated on activities within the confines of Three Rivers Stadium, but instead were drawn downtown, to the U. S. Court and Post Office building. There, on Grant Street, under the glare of cameras from the three major networks, *U.S. v Strong* was striking a severe blow to the well being of the National Pastime.

A portly former caterer, Curtis Strong, was on trial for a more iniquitous vocation, the distribution of illicit drugs. It was Strong's clientele, major-league baseball players, that brought an attentive and appalled nation to the Courthouse doorsteps. The "Pittsburgh Drug Trial" was baseball's darkest hour since the Black Sox scandal of 1919. In some eyes, Strong was seen as a latter-day Arnold Rothstein, the fixer of the '19 Series. Perhaps "Chef" Curtis was Rothstein incarnate.

The Black Sox committed the ultimate baseball sin; they lost the World Series *on purpose.* A boundless lust for the dollar became more important than the players' own integrity. Still, in recent years, the eight members of the White Sox who conspired to throw the 1919 Series have been romanticized to some degree.

Concerns that the witnesses in the 1985 Pittsburgh drug trials will someday be viewed in the same light as Shoeless Joe Jackson should be cast aside. The ugliness that would spew from the court during those two weeks began with defense attorney Adam Renfroe's opening statement. Renfroe told the jury that the major league players who would come before them as witnesses were "nothing but junkies."[60]

"They are no different than the element in the Hill [District], on Fifth Avenue, in Homewood, the South Side and the North Side." Renfroe opined. "The only difference is that they make hundreds of thousands of dollars."[61] In his zeal to defend his client, Renfroe had decided to put major league baseball on trial, and no team took a harder hit than the Pittsburgh Pirates, and no player more so than Dave Parker.

Stimulants, legal and illegal, have a long and storied history in the game of baseball. Babe Ruth, Hack Wilson, Grover Cleveland Alexander, Paul Waner — Hall of Famers all — enjoyed their fair share of adult beverages ... often to excess. Baseball lore is full of entertaining tales of players executing great feats while under the influence, or while recovering from a terrific bout with the bottle. Alcohol, though the most common intoxicant among ballplayers, has by no means been the sole choice for big leaguers.

The use of amphetamines in the major leagues had been public knowledge since Jim Bouton wrote of "greenies" in his best-selling memoir, *Ball Four.* When published in 1970, *Ball Four* shocked naïve readers with a number of startling revelations. Included in the text were disclosures that some ballplayers enjoyed the company of attractive young women while on the road; that some star players (e.g., Mickey Mantle) don't always treat their adoring fans well; and that a number of players regularly used amphetamines to enhance their performance.

In an interview with *Playboy* in 1979, Pete Rose acknowledged the use of an occasional greenie. "...If a doctor gives me a prescription of thirty diet pills, because I want to curb my appetite, so I can lose five pounds before I go to spring training, I mean is that bad?" Rose rhetorically asked his inquisitor. "I mean, a doctor is not going to write a prescription that is going to be harmful to my body. A lot of guys might think there are days you might need a greenie, an upper.... I might have taken a greenie last week."[62]

A man less forthright with the truth than Rose might be difficult to believe, but others corroborated his and Bouton's accounts that amphetamine use is common in baseball. While under oath at the Pittsburgh drug trial, both Dale Berra and John Milner spoke freely of their own experience with amphetamines. Each man made headlines by implicating iconic figures of the game during their testimony.

"I heard that if I wanted one (a greenie) I would go ask them (Willie Stargell and Bill Madlock)." Berra said from the stand. "I never asked them, I'm not sure they would give me one even.'[63]

The invocation of Stargell's name shook the baseball world. Stargell's popularity extended beyond his adopted hometown of Pittsburgh, Willie was revered throughout the baseball world. Certainly, he couldn't be involved in this sordid drug mess. However, the shocking developments didn't end with Berra's statement. John Milner, a member of the Pirates in the late seventies, recalled another baseball legend possessing amphetamines when he was with the New York Mets.

"Management wasn't giving me greenies or speed. Willie (Mays) had the red juice. I went into his locker and got it." However, Milner added, "I never saw him take it."[64]

Stargell was succinct and to the point when asked about the charges. "I've never seen anyone distribute any drugs of any kind in the clubhouse." Willie said in 1985, while a coach with the Bucs. "There's no truth to it at all. When there's no truth to a matter, there is nothing to comment."[65]

As expected, Mays also denied acquaintance with any substance stronger than coffee. "I'm not involved in anything like that," The Say Hey Kid innocently claimed. "I don't use speed. I don't even know what it is and I don't know what he (Milner) is talking about."[66]

A good many fans believed the protestations of these two baseball legends. However, Stargell's and Mays's straight-faced claims of innocence would have been easier to swallow if one hadn't known of the widespread use of the drug throughout the game. On the heels of a labor dispute that resulted in a one-day work stoppage in August, the game certainly didn't need its heroes attacked. If guilty, Willie and Willie had committed minor infractions, but the matter wasn't pressed; the stature of our heroes remained intact. A savory news story was taking place on Grant Street, and the media had other, less revered targets to zero in on.

The first witnesses in the trial startled the public with their raw testimony. A shaken Keith Hernandez recounted his addiction, and remembered awakening one morning: "...my nose was bleeding, I was having the shakes." The New York Mets' first baseman estimated that "40 percent"[67] of all big league players used cocaine in 1980, a season he described as "the love affair year," between the drug and players.

Parker's name entered the headlines following the testimony of Los Angeles Dodger Enos Cabell. "**Used Cocaine with Parker, Dodger Player Says,**" read the bold type above the fold, where Dave's name would remain in the Pittsburgh dailies throughout the next few days. Following Cabell's account, in which he revealed that he had snorted cocaine with Parker in a Pittsburgh hotel, Dave publicly acknowledged his use of the drug for the first time.

Dale Berra, a former teammate of Dave's, was the next to testify, and he too implicated Parker.

"Who first introduced you to cocaine?" Renfroe asked Berra.

"Dave Parker, John Milner." Berra answered.

Attempting to pass Parker off as the criminal in place of Strong, Renfroe continued, "Would you tell the jury about that occasion?"

"One time in Puerto Rico, " Berra replied, " I happened to ask Dave Parker if he used the drug before. He did not want to answer me at that time. When I got back to the hotel, a door opened on the opposite side of my room and Dave Parker said, 'Does this answer your question?' He had it [cocaine] on him."[68]

With the testimony of Berra and Cabell safely on the record, the demonization of Parker was complete. The city's vilification of Dave was now, in the eyes of his detractors, justified. When he finally took the stand on September 11, the distaste many Pittsburgh fans felt for Parker had only intensified. Although his testimony wasn't nearly as dramatic as Hernandez's, the *Pittsburgh Post-Gazette* played up his appearance with a banner front-page headline. "Parker Used Cocaine for Three Years."

Under oath, David informed the court that he had first tried cocaine in 1976, when he was playing winter ball in Venezuela. However, it wasn't until 1979 that he began using cocaine "with consistency," Parker confessed. The drug was then "becoming vastly popular in society and it was constantly available because of who I was."[69]

Curtis Strong entered Parker's life in 1980 when Dave met the defendant in the hotel room of visiting Los Angeles Dodgers, but it wasn't until the off season of 1981 that Parker first bought cocaine from Strong. The initial exchange took place at a motel a week before Christmas. The second transaction happened at a New Year's Eve party held at Bill Madlock's home. "Most of the Pittsburgh Pirates knew him (Strong) and it was a team party."[70] Dave said.

On cross-examination Adam Renfroe brought up the name of Shelby Greer, a former Pittsburgher who had been charged with ten counts of distributing cocaine between 1979 and 1985. Under Renfroe's barrage of questions, Dave admitted that he had met Greer following the '79 Series on a flight from Pittsburgh to Denver, when he was en route to Japan for an All-Star game. According to Parker, Greer presented himself "as an oil and gas man out of Denver."[71]

In time, Parker learned that he could procure cocaine though Greer. The dealer occasionally traveled on team flights, and had free access to the team's clubhouse. Renfroe used this information to vigorously attack Parker with a cross-examination so malevolent one could easily have mistaken the lawyer for a patron of Three Rivers' right-field stands.

"Because of his free access, all of these young guys who looked up to you bought cocaine from Shelby Greer ... and wrecked their career. How can you carry that burden?" the attorney asked.

"I don't carry any burden," Parker replied. "I don't feel I was responsible for them. I can't take responsibility for what another adult does with his life."

Renfroe, apparently suffering from a brief loss of hearing, continued. "How do you feel being responsible for young kids wrecking their career, young kids who looked up to you?"

"I don't have any feelings." Parker reiterated. "I don't think I'm responsible."

That response didn't deter the defense attorney's dogged vilification of the witness. "You don't care, do you, Mr. Parker? You only care about yourself."

"Of course I care about Dale Berra and Rod Scurry," David asserted. "They are personal friends of mine, but they are adults.... I do not take responsibility for that."

The badgering of the witness still didn't cease. "You facilitated their using drugs. How could you facilitate their drug use when these young players looked up to you, a veteran, Mr. Parker?"

"I introduced him (Greer) as a gas and oil man,"[72] came Parker's feeble response.

David survived his ordeal in court. He left Pittsburgh, caught up with his teammates in Cincinnati, and went on an incredible hitting tear. Over the course of the final five weeks of the season, Parker hit .384 with 11 home runs and 38 RBI's. While Dave was ripping the cover off the ball, Renfroe was again invoking his name in Pittsburgh.

"If Dave Parker didn't have immunity, he'd be going to jail for 150 years," the attorney told news hounds gathered outside the courthouse. The next day, in his closing argument, Renfroe continued to attempt to deflect blame from his client. "If this is the guy who's destroying the spinal cord of America [baseball], put him in jail; put him away. But I suggest he is not the one destroying the spinal cord of America; it's the ballplayers, the managers and the owners with all the money that are using him as a scapegoat.

"Ladies and gentleman, it's the haves against the have-nots. In a few years there won't be any more middle class. It's either you're going to have plenty or you're not going to have it at all."[73]

Renfroe's defense of Strong did his client no good. Chef Curtis was found guilty, but the counselor was successful in his attempt to vilify the witnesses/ballplayers. The game had been sullied.

Peter Ueberroth had become the commissioner of baseball in 1985, after Bowie Kuhn was muscled out of the position by several powerful owners. In Ueberroth the owners had laid claim to a man with an ego that could match even the most vainglorious in their assemblage. With his successful and profitable management of the Los Angeles Olympics, Ueberroth became the most sought-after commodity in the corporate world, and being named *Time* magazine's Man of The Year for 1984 only helped his negotiating position. Before accepting the position of commissioner, Peter demanded, and ultimately received, complete authority over the game.

The lords of the game certainly didn't have the foresight to recognize what this concession would spell for them when labor strife hit the game in the summer of '85. On August 6 the Player's Association, under the leadership of Donald Fehr, went on strike. The strike lasted but one day, thanks to the commissioner's intervention in the negotiating process. Ueberroth was so frantic in his belief that the labor strife would stain his magnificent record that he stepped on the toes of management's negotiating team, which led to another victory for the Player's Association. Ueberroth's apparent leadership earned him great kudos from the public for his intervention.

Though he was publicly viewed as a hero for aborting the strike, Peter had angered many in management with his grandstanding. Some in the media lauded him for standing up to the owners, among them Bob Smizik of the *Pittsburgh Press*.

"One of Ueberroth's greatest attributes as commissioner is he has no fear of the owners," Smizik wrote. "His star is so firmly established in this country—first for giving us the best Olympics ever, and then for helping settle the baseball strike—he has no fear of losing his job."[74]

Armed with his sweeping authority, and a pocket full of press clippings, Ueberroth moved next to decide what punishment to mete out to the game's admitted drug users. Ueberroth, who by this time fancied himself as a better coiffed version of Kenesaw Landis, moved with great deliberation. In a move reminiscent of Landis's most famous ruling that banned Chicago's Black Sox, Peter announced the punishment of seven "class I" chemical abusers in the game, of which Dave Parker was one.

To play in 1986, Parker would be forced to give 10 percent of his $1.2-million salary to anti-drug programs, and contribute two hundred hours of his time to community service over the span of two years.

David, understandably, was not pleased to hear of Ueberroth's directive. "I find it odd that some of the players who received only "class II" punishment from the commissioner were using drugs as recently as last year," Parker said. "My use of cocaine ended five years ago. Isn't there a five-year statute of limitations on everything except murder? I think the commissioner's action was just a political play to force a drug-testing plan for baseball."[75]

Parker's comments could easily be dismissed as sour grapes had Ueberroth evenhandedly distributed the punishment. Instead, to echo Adam Renfroe, the commissioner used the Pittsburgh witnesses as scapegoats. Baseball's drug problems went much deeper than Curtis Strong's customers, but Ueberroth's uneven penalization gave no acknowledgment of that fact.

As ordered by Ueberroth, Dave donated the $120,000 to a number of charities in the Cincinnati neighborhood where he grew up. Parker, in acquiescing to the directive, admitted that, had he been running the game, choosing the proper punishment would not have been easy. "What kind of action would I have decided to take if I had been in the commissioner's shoes?" Dave rhetorically asked. "I have to admit that I don't know. [76]"

One thing is certain: whatever the punishment Czar Parker would have dealt out, it wouldn't have been so harsh ... or expensive. "Obviously it's a pretty damned large fine, and I'm pretty angry about it. But I'll pay it, and it will still be worth every penny of that $120,000 if, by doing so, I can put all this behind me."[77]

Surely Parker had to know that, given his past history, nothing could have been that easy. Kick an addiction, be forced to admit the addiction in front of the entire world, have a punitive ruling against you, and still the ordeal wouldn't be over.

The Pittsburgh Pirates, backed by team president Malcom Prine, sued Parker for the remainder of the salary he was owed in deferred payments. The Pirates charged that Parker had deceived the club by concealing his drug use, and had misrepresented his condition at the time of negotiations in 1979. The team contended that "the deterioration of Parker's skills as a baseball player and his failure to stay in good physical condition while under the contract he signed in '79 were directly related to, and caused by, his improper, illegal, and heavy use of cocaine."[78]

It was Dave's own words during his testimony in the drug trial that opened the door for the suit. "I had a daughter. She was more important than cocaine," he explained of kicking his drug habit. "I wanted to get married and that was more important than cocaine. It was a matter of choice.... I stopped in the late part of the 1982 season. I felt my game was slipping and I felt it (cocaine) played a part in it."[79]

The basis for the suit centered around Section 4B of the standard player's contract, which stated that "no player shall knowingly hide from club officials a physical or mental defect that could impair his performance."

"The Pirates were deprived of that which he promised to provide," Prine said. "The basis for our lawsuit rests on the fact that during and after the signing of the contract that gives rise to our future payments, he was using cocaine that materially affected his ability to perform, and the Pittsburgh Pirates were deprived of that which he promised to provide. We therefore are asking the courts to declare the contract null and void and we be relieved of future payments."[80]

As would be expected, Dave disagreed with the Pirates' position. "I signed a contract to play baseball in Pittsburgh for five years, not to win five batting titles and five MVP's ... they couldn't afford me and that was one of the reasons I deferred money. If I had known then what I know now, I'd have been sure to take all the money up front.... I hate the fact that they say they didn't get their money's worth out of me when I was considered the best player in baseball for six of the ten years I was there."[81]

Though the decision to sue Parker was popular with a public fed up with an athletic world which was perceived to be dominated by prima donnas, there were many questions about the merits of the lawsuit.

The Pirates did not attempt to be reimbursed for money already paid to Parker under the contract. Nor did the club attempt to sue other Pittsburgh players who had testified under oath to the use of cocaine while under contract to the Pirates. Had Pittsburgh's argument been warranted, should they not have pursued those avenues as well? Why hadn't other clubs sued their narcotic-abusing players? The answer to that query: Pittsburgh/Parker was a unique predicament.

Dave was gone from Pittsburgh at the time of the suit and the Pirates no longer needed to avoid offending a player currently performing for them. The franchise was in dire financial straits and cancelling a $5-million debt burden would be a great relief to the club. More importantly, public approval was clearly on the club's side. Parker was viewed by many in the Steel City as a miscreant when he left the Pirates following the '83 season, and his testimony at the Strong trial only reinforced these beliefs. A jury trial in Pittsburgh would weigh heavily in favor of the Bucs. Proof of management's belief in this theory lay in the fact that the team bypassed provisions in the Basic Agreement by filing a civil suit, rather than pursuing a grievance against Parker.

A trial would surely bring much attention and notoriety, but the Pirates still pressed on. The team had a lengthy potential witness list that included a number of ex–Bucs, former commissioner Bowie Kuhn, Pirates owner Dan Galbreath, and Dave's children. Prine and others in Pirates management obviously weren't content with the ugliness of the Strong trial; they welcomed the opportunity to drag the franchise and the game through the mud again ... if it meant saving the cash-strapped team a substantial amount of money.

The breach-of-contract suit was settled out of court shortly before a date was set for trial in December 1988. Tom Reich, Parker's agent, believed that the settlement was in the best interests of his client. "The jury trial in Pittsburgh was far more compelling (for settlement) than the merits of the claim,"[82] Reich acceded.

Carl Barger, the club's president in '88, and Prine's partner in hatching the suit, offered an olive branch to the team's former right fielder. "We said all along this wasn't a personal vendetta against Dave Parker. It was a matter of principle and economics,"[83] Barger claimed.

Lynching aren't often personal vendetta either; but the lawsuit, following Ueberroth's judgment, smacked of persecution. Despite Barger's insistence to the contrary, the suit was clearly a vindictive act. Parker, though no innocent himself, found himself a victim of baseball's ruling class.

Thank U for Lettin' Me Be Myself Agin

"What went down in Pittsburgh is stored in my memory bank," Parker said after leaving the Pirates. "I'll never forget it. It later made me a better man to know something like that, racial-prejudice, still exists in Pittsburgh. I was big and Black. I was outspoken because I believed in myself. I won a batting title and predicted I'd win it again; then I did it. Fans interpreted that as a Black man with a big ego who was vain. Pete Rose has done that for twenty-two years, and fans think it's great. With him, they praised his competitive fire and his confidence."[84]

Once the '83 season ended, Parker wasted little time officially dissolving his relationship with the Pittsburgh Pirates. On December 7 Dave signed a two-year, $2.6 million contract with the Cincinnati Reds. Parker arrived at the press conference that announced his signing wearing a bright red carnation, to "celebrate my going home."[85]

"This is like a transfusion," Parker said. "This is very exciting for me, and I know it's going to motivate me and stimulate me as an individual. I'm healthy, and I'm looking for big productions out of myself."[86]

Dave responded well to his new environment. He led the 1984 Reds in every major offensive category: home runs (16), RBI's (94), hits (173), doubles (28), and game-winning RBI's (13).

Parker's second year in Cincinnati was even more impressive than the first. Practically singlehandedly Dave carried the Reds to an unexpected second-place finish in the National League's western division. On a personal level, Dave finished second to the Cardinals' Willie McGee in balloting for Most Valuable Player.

"It wasn't my best season. That had to be 1978," Parker said. "And my team didn't win a world championship like it did in 1979. But I sure had more fun in 1985 than I did in any other year."[87]

Pete Rose, Parker's manager, believed that Dave, rather than McGee, should have got the MVP. "I have been around a lot of MVP's during my career, including myself," Rose said. "I played with John Bench, Joe Morgan, George Foster and Mike Schmidt. None meant more to the team in the year they won it than Dave Parker did to us this season."[88]

Dave Parker at home with the Cincinnati Reds (author's collection).

As his career wound down, Parker suffered the same fate as many Black stars in the game; he was bounced from team to team, and despite still being a contributing factor, was forced into early retirement. Dave's rebirth in Cincinnati lasted four years. Following the '87 season Parker was traded to the Oakland A's. Two seasons in Oakland were followed by a year in Milwaukee and a season split between California and Toronto.

Though his talent was on the downside, Dave remained an intimidating presence at the plate. His career came to a close in 1992 with Dave sitting at 2,712 hits, just shy of his personal goal of 3,000 and probably an automatic nomination to the Hall of Fame.

"My goal was to play this year, and if there is a season next year, to play and get my 3,000 hits," Parker said. "But I was tossed out when I was still a productive player. It doesn't happen for the Black players like it does for the white boys, though. Name the Black players that were allowed to reach major goals. Not a lot.

"When Pete Rose was going for Ty Cobb's record, Pete was not a valuable part of that Reds lineup at the time. But it just doesn't happen for the Black player. It might not be what people want to hear, but these are the realities, facts. I'm saying it because I lived it," Parker said.

"I'm proud of the fact that I can say 'I revolutionized the salary structure in baseball.' But I paid for it. I caught the wrath of being the first."[89]

6

Thank You, But You Missed the Show: *Barry Bonds*

> When you're good you're supposed to be humble. Sometimes I think people don't like me because I enjoy being this good too much.[1]
>
> Barry Bonds

One could say he was destined for greatness. After all, given his bloodline, the fact that Barry Bonds would become one of the greatest baseball players of all time came as scant surprise to close observers.

Bonds's father, Bobby, was one of the premier talents in baseball during the decade of the seventies. The senior Bonds arrived in the major leagues with the San Francisco Giants in 1968 at the age of twenty-two. While with the Giants, Bobby displayed a remarkable blend of power and speed. In his first full season, Bonds belted 32 home runs and drove in 90 runs, while scoring 120 and swiping 45 bases. After his outstanding debut season Bobby was considered the heir apparent to teammate Willie Mays.

"I would never say I was better than everybody else," the elder Bonds said in retirement. "But there was nothing on the field that *anybody* could do that I couldn't do."[2]

Bonds's words may ring of conceit, but his career statistics bear out his statement. In fourteen big-league seasons, Bobby drove in 1,024 runs, hit 332 home runs, stole 461 bases, and scored 1,258 runs. Perhaps most impressive of all Bonds's career highlights were his five 30/30 seasons—that is, thirty home runs and thirty steals in the same campaign—a major-league record. For Bonds, though, all the notable numbers took a backseat to nagging criticism that followed him throughout his career.

Barry Bonds: "I want to be remembered as the best left fielder ever to play baseball" (© **AFP/CORBIS**).

A teammate was anonymously quoted as saying that Bobby never stole a meaningful base, and that he couldn't hit a cut-off man even if his target were "King Kong." Also, receiving as much attention as his home runs and stolen bases were Bonds's high strikeout totals. Bobby finished his career third on the all-time strikeout list, and set a single-season record with 189 whiffs in 1970.

Among the notable facets of Bonds's career was the frequency with which he changed teams. After a seven-year stint with the Giants, Bobby played for seven different teams in the final seven years of his career. Why was such a productive and talented asset shuttled from one club to the next? The answer, vague as it may seem, is that Bonds was viewed as a malcontent ... a malady that struck Black athletes more often than not.

Baseball's decision makers, and the men who covered the game, recognized Bonds's talent. However, Bobby's accomplishments were vastly under appreciated by these same men, a fact not missed by Bonds's first-born son, Barry.

"No one gives my dad credit for what he did...," Barry complained "[He] did 30/30 five times, and they say he never became the ballplayer he should have become. Ain't nobody else done 30/30 five times. *Nobody*."[3]

"*Unfulfilled potential.*" It was an albatross that burdened the father and would hinder the son.

Barry was born on July 24, 1964, to Pat and Bobby Bonds. With his father as role model, Barry naturally gravitated to the game of baseball.

As a child Barry would spend afternoons playing with the offspring of his father's teammates. While Barry's father and his godfather, Willie Mays, were performing on Candlestick Park's playing field, the younger Bonds was playing his own brand of baseball. Along with the children of Gaylord Perry, Juan Marichal, and Tito Fuentes, among others, Bonds would crush empty beer cups, mold them into a sphere, and swat the makeshift "ball" about the locker room with small Bat Day giveaway bats.

Those sessions in the Candlestick clubhouse served Barry well. Upon his graduation from high school, San Francisco drafted Bonds in the second round of the 1982 draft. Barry turned down the Giants' offer of $75,000 and opted instead to attend Arizona State University, the alma mater of his cousin Reggie Jackson.

While starring with the Sun Devils, Barry developed a good relationship with his coach, Jim Brock, but the same could not be said about his ASU teammates. "Unfortunately I never saw a teammate care about him," Brock said. "Part of it would be his being rude, inconsiderate and self-centered. He bragged about the money he turned down, and he popped off about his dad. I don't think he ever figured out what to do to get people to like him."

Brock wouldn't be the last to make such an assertion. However, Barry's personality shortcomings could usually be overshadowed by his ability. "I've had lots of kids with enormous talent," Brock said. "But the thing that separated Barry from the pack is his total love for the game. It's all he talked about, all he lived for."[4]

In three years under Brock, Bonds put up spectacular numbers. His collegiate efforts were rewarded when the Pittsburgh Pirates picked him in the sixth round of the 1985 free-agent draft.

Talent Takes Care of Everything ... Great Talent Comes to the Surface.[5]

"Barry is one of those guys who comes along every once in awhile who can put some people in the stands," Pittsburgh Pirate manager Jim Leyland observed. "He's strong mentally and emotionally. Combine those two with God-given talent and it's hard to beat."[6]

Leyland showed great faith in Barry by making the twenty-one-year-old his lead-off hitter immediately upon the rookie's arrival on May 30, 1986. Bonds's minor-league experience was limited: Half a year at Class A Prince William saw Bonds hit .299, belt 13 home runs, and accumulate 37 RBI's.

Barry arrived at Pittsburgh's '86 spring training camp as a non-roster invitee. Despite a strong showing during the spring season, Leyland and Pittsburgh general manager Syd Thrift opted to send Barry to Triple-A for another year of seasoning. Just a month and a half into the '86 campaign, Bonds was batting .311 for Hawaii when Thrift flew to Arizona in order to assess Pittsburgh's number-one prospect. Prior to an evening contest, Thrift observed Bonds pull half a dozen pitches over the right field wall. The Pirate G.M. sat unmoved.

"Any good hitter can do that," he told Bonds. "I'd like to see you hit a few over the left field fence."

Barry stepped back into the batter's box and proceeded to hit five straight deliveries over the left field wall.

"Is that good enough for you?" Bonds asked Thrift with a grin.[7]

The rhetorical question was answered later that evening when Thrift instructed the Hawaiian manager to pull the prodigy from that night's game in the fifth inning. Barry's minor-league career had come to a close. Within hours he was on a plane headed for Pittsburgh.

Less than a year after becoming the sixth pick in the '85 free-agent draft, Barry Bonds was leading off and playing center field for the Pirates. Within a week of his big league debut, Bonds would face New York Mets ace Dwight Gooden. What did he think about batting against Gooden? members of the press asked Barry.

"He's going to have to face *me*,"[8] Bonds brashly responded. Such remarks made Bonds a ripe subject for the men who covered the Pirates.

"I feel the press puts a stamp on certain players and once they stamp you as a 'bad person' then that's what they feed on and there's nothing you can do about it," Bonds said later. "I know in my heart the type of ball player I am and the type of person I am.

"As many people as they say don't like you, I have that many people who do like me, so I don't worry about it."[9]

Barry's early days in the major leagues were played in the shadow of his father's legacy. Reporters would sometimes slip and refer to him as "Bobby." These innocent mistakes frustrated and angered the young man striving to leave his own mark.

"I don't mind being compared [to his father] I just don't want it to be an everyday question," Barry would say. "I love my family dearly. It's just that this gets old after awhile."[10]

Pressure to match his father's performance perhaps affected Bonds early in his career. Barry batted just .223, .261, .283, and .248 in his first four seasons, numbers that fell well below expectations for the former number one draft pick.

"The national media created expectations that were totally unrealistic," Bonds asserted. "People wanted a superstar right from Jump Street; people wouldn't get off me for just being good."[11]

Finally, in the 1990 season, Barry surpassed "just being good," and fulfilled even the grandest predictions made of him. During the off season prior to the '90 campaign, Bonds spent five days a week working out under the supervision of Dr. Warren Sipp. Barry's strenuous conditioning program certainly helped strengthen him for the long grueling season, but he also had matured a great deal as a player. As a lead-off man, Barry was often over-anxious and prone to swinging at bad pitches. Beginning in 1990, Leyland dropped Barry to the number-five spot where a more patient and deliberate Bonds paid immediate dividends for his manager's ingenuity.

"This was the year I wanted to hit .300," Barry said at the time. "I was going to stay away from home runs, just beat the ball into the ground and use my speed ... and then everything came together at once. That was a shocking surprise."[12]

Barry batted .301, hit 33 home runs, stole 53 bases and drove in 114 runs while leading the Pirates to the National League playoffs. Though the Cincinnati Reds defeated Pittsburgh in the post season, Bonds's excellent year was acknowledged. Barry captured 23 out of 24 first-place votes for the National League Most Valuable Player award. *The Sporting News* also honored him as the 1990 Major League Player of the Year.

"For, like everybody? The American League too?" Barry asked when informed of the award.

Once he was assured that, indeed, the award was for the best player in all the game, Bonds displayed an unusual bit of humility.

"That's pretty cool," he said with an appreciative smile.[13]

During the course of the Cincinnati playoff series, Bonds displayed a less endearing aspect of his personality. Prior to game five of the series, Pirates third baseman Jeff King pulled himself from the lineup due to a back injury.

"He's a young player," Bonds told reporters of King. "He should be out there. Sooner or later he'll come out of it, but if he doesn't someone is going to take his job ... Jeff King can sit there and get his back ready for spring training."[14]

Barry's insensitive comments drew the ire of a number of teammates. His callous and flippant remarks portrayed a self-centered jerk, and Barry did little to dispel any such notion.

"Barry can be arrogant; he can really tick you off at times," R.J. Reynolds, a former teammate of Bonds, said. "One day he's the greatest person in the world, and the next day he won't talk to you, but a lot of it is an act."[15]

The following spring a highly publicized incident in training camp did little to ingratiate an already unpopular Bonds to either his teammates or the fans of Pittsburgh.

Barry came to spring training fresh off a loss at the arbitration table. Bonds had failed to prove his case and was forced to settle for $2.3 million rather than the $3.3 million yearly salary he sought. Though Barry later insisted that the arbitration case had nothing to do with the episode, the media read the situation differently.

"I had a friend who came to Florida to take pictures of me," Bonds explained. "I paid for him to be there. A camera guy from the media came up to my face. And I asked him to move. He didn't want to move. I physically moved him from my sight."[16]

Pirates public relations man Jim Lachimia saw the altercation and walked over to Bonds, "If that camera man can't stay, your guy can't stay," he told Barry.

Seeing Bonds exchange words with Lachima, Pittsburgh coach Bill Virdon stepped in to aid the P.R. man. Barry then lashed out at Virdon, prompting Jim Leyland, who saw the commotion from a distance, to defend his coach.

With cameras rolling, Leyland railed against his M.V.P. left fielder. "I've kissed your butt for three years," Leyland shouted. "No one player is going to ruin this camp. If you don't want to be here, then get your butt off the field."[17]

The blowup at McKechnie Field led off that evening's sportscast, and was played *ad nauseam* for several days thereafter. For the press, the encounter between manger and player presented a perfect opportunity to display the egotism of the modern athlete. The audience relished Leyland's on-camera reprimand of the prima donna. To the public the ugly exchange was another example of a spoiled millionaire pushing the limits of acceptable behavior. Bonds was already held in low esteem by a majority of Pittsburgh's paying customers. By shoving a working, properly credentialed, cameraman, Barry only widened the chasm between players and fans.

In the weeks following the incident, Barry's production on the field suffered. Everywhere he turned, and in every city the Pirates visited, Bonds was reminded of the McKechnie Field altercation. Only when Leyland intervened with the press did Barry's fortunes rebound.

"Leave him alone," the Buc manager instructed the local media. "With all that Barry Bonds has brought to this city, it's time to get off his back."[18]

"I respect his job, he respects my job. I love Jim Leyland," Bonds said shortly after the episode. "I think he's the greatest manager I ever played for. He's the greatest guy I ever played for."[19]

Barry quickly bounced back from his slow start and again led the Pirates to the Eastern division title. On this occasion, Pittsburgh's opponent was the Atlanta Braves, but the results were the same as the previous year's. Atlanta advanced to the World Series while the Pirates went home again, disappointed that their ultimate goal was not achieved.

On a personal level, Barry also fell short in '91 when he placed second in the Most Valuable Player voting to Atlanta's Terry Pendleton. A glance at the statistics of the two men show that it's conceivable that had Bonds practiced better press relations he might very well have garnered his second MVP.

	Avg.	*HR*	*RBI*	*R*
Bonds	.292	25	116	109
Pendleton	.311	21	105	94

Bonds won a Gold Glove for the '91 season; Pendleton did not.

"I don't like to talk to a whole lot of reporters, because, number one, I already know what the questions are going to be ... about my father ... about how the team feels ... about how good the other team is going to be," Bonds remarked.

"I don't like to get involved in those things. I just like to go to work and then go home. I just like being that quiet horse. So I've had this stamp on me that I'm a bad person and hard to deal with."[20]

Perhaps the writers were correct in selecting the Atlanta third baseman as MVP. Pendleton certainly enjoyed an exemplary year; however, one could also interpret the numbers in Bonds's favor. For some voters, though, Barry's Gold Glove and great offensive statistics were cast aside. In their eyes, Bonds was a detriment to the game. He was "a symbol of baseball's greed and selfishness, complete with diamond earring."[21]

Despite the fact that Bonds would be eligible for free agency following the 1992 season, the Pirates refused to seriously negotiate a long-term deal with their left fielder. On the pretext that Pittsburgh was a small market, the franchise had a built in excuse not to retain Bonds. Justified or not, the club took full advantage of the "small market" argument, and made only a token offer to Bonds. The tempestuous slugger would play his seventh season in Pittsburgh with the knowledge that it would be his last.

For the third consecutive season the Pirates finished atop their division, and for the second straight year they faced Atlanta in the post season. Again, as in '91 and '92, the Pirates' campaign ended in disappointment

The Pirates held a 2–0 lead as the seventh and deciding game entered the bottom of the ninth inning. Terry Pendleton led off the inning with a double and moved to third when the next batter, David Justice, reached first via an error by second baseman Jose Lind. A walk to Sid Bream loaded the bases for Atlanta, who then scored their first run of the game on a sacrifice fly by Ron Gant. Another walk, this time by Damon Berryhill, reloaded the bases. The second out came when Brian Hunter popped up, leaving the game in the hands of pinch-hitter Francisco Cabrera. An unlikely hero, Cabrera delivered nonetheless, with a line-drive single to left.

Bonds, who was playing a deep left field because of two previously hit long foul balls, had to charge the base hit. Barry gathered up the ball and made a strong throw to the plate. The ball, however, arrived a moment too late, as Sid Bream lumbered around third and across the plate with the pennant-winning run.

While the Braves joyously rushed the field and enveloped Bream at home plate, Bonds sat in disbelief on the Fulton County Stadium turf. The Pirates' three-year run at the Series had come to an agonizing close. Also, for the third straight year Barry had failed to produce at the plate during the championship series. His cumulative average for the trio of playoff appearances was a miserable .191.

Barry's second MVP winning season was largely overlooked in light of his sub-par playoff performance. The fact that Bonds was leaving Pittsburgh was a foregone conclusion. Where he would next lace up his spikes was the only unanswered question. The speculation ended several weeks after the conclusion of the World Series. In early December, Barry signed the richest contract in baseball history with the San Francisco Giants. For the princely sum of $43.75 million, Barry Bonds would now ply his trade on the nation's left coast.

Tell Me Something I Can't Do, and I'll Show You I Can Do It.[22]

With his place as one of the game's finest players secure, Barry no longer fled the legacy of his father and godfather. Upon signing with the Giants, Bonds sought, and received, permission to wear Willie Mays's retired number 24. Bonds had already worn the number as a Pirate in honor of Mays, but wearing the same number in San Francisco was quite another thing.

Despite having the blessing of Mays, Bonds found himself widely criticized by sport columnists across the country. "Plastering Mays' No. 24

on Bonds' overpriced back is going to be an open invitation for ridicule for someone who already faces impossible expectations,"[23] Tom Weir wrote in *USA Today.*

Following several days of increased pressure, Barry relented on his wish and opted instead to don number 25, his father's jersey number with the Giants. While a younger Bonds would turn cold when asked about his father, the new Barry openly embraced the linkage between father and son.

"I want to put my father and myself in an untouchable class as a father-son combination," Barry told reporters. "I want us to be the best ever in baseball."[24] The elder Bonds would be able to witness Barry's assault on the history books firsthand: San Francisco's new manager, Dusty Baker, had named Bobby the club's batting coach.

And what a sight Barry was to behold in '93! His initial season in a Giant uniform was arguably the finest ever put forth by a player in the aftermath of a large free agent signing. For the third time in four seasons, Bonds was selected as the Most Valuable Player of the National League, an unprecedented achievement.

In spite of his new locale and his continued brilliance on the field, Barry's strained relationship with the media continued. A high-profile *Sports Illustrated* cover story did little to rehabilitate Bonds's already dreadful public persona. Over the course of nine pages the magazine article intricately detailed the amount of time Barry kept a reporter waiting for an interview.

"Hey, if the press paid me, I'd be giving interviews all day," Bonds said on one occasion. "They don't. They come around all the time before games, when I have to stretch, think about the game, get ready to do my job. So a lot of times I won't talk. Maybe they get mad, so they write that way."[25]

Perhaps more than any other player, Bonds epitomized the widening gap between players and the press corps. Barry viewed the media as an unnecessary nuisance; the press believed Bonds walked through each day with a colossal chip on his shoulder.

Bonds refused to recognize the part that the working press played in promoting the game ... promotion which, in turn, increased revenue and helped make his exorbitant salary possible.

"[Bonds] made it very clear in his first season with the Giants that he didn't consider doing media interviews part of his job," a San Francisco official conveyed. "He made it pretty clear that isn't what he's paid to do. He doesn't subscribe to the philosophy that it's part of the job to deal with the public or the media away from the field. No matter how we slice it, that's the way he feels."[26]

The ill-tempered Bonds once described his give-and-take with the press in a particularly unflattering way. "I thrive off you guys," he told several gathered writers, "because I love to make you come to my locker begging."[27]

"You know what my plan is?" he asked on another occasion. " Just to wear out all the people who like to get down on me. Just wear their asses out. I want them to be thinking, 'Damn that Barry just shuts me up every single season. Okay, we still think he's a little arrogant. We still think he's a little flashy. But it's just finally reached the point where we can't say nothing about the boy's ball.' 'Cause there ain't no shame in my game."[28]

Barry's game may have been lacking in "shame," but his actions, such as shoving a writer from *USA Today*, were indefensible. The rancor displayed in the print media stemmed from just such actions. As much as certain members of the press may have disliked Bonds on a personal level, through, Barry's skills were rarely questioned.

"When Bonds pops off, he sounds self-serving and petulant," Jerry Crasnick wrote in *Baseball America*. "The public perception of him is essentially dead-on."[29]

Crasnick continued, "You can't help but marvel at the man's skills. He plays hard — except when he's standing at home plate admiring a home run — and he never begs out of the lineup.... Everyone respects Bonds the ballplayer. But sportswriters aren't the only ones tired of his moodiness. If you think he's universally beloved in the clubhouse, you haven't surveyed any of his former teammates today."[30]

Feuds between the press and sporting heroes were not a new phenomenon. Many in the media regarded greats like Joe Di Maggio and Ted Williams as sullen and boorish. Like Bonds, Williams was believed to be a "spoiled brat" when he arrived in the major leagues. Also, like Barry, the "Splendid Splinter" continued his feud with the press long after he established himself as a superstar, using perceived slights from his younger days as fodder for his fury.

While Williams played in an era and a city dominated by newsprint, Bonds's career coincided with the great proliferation of cable sports networks. Beginning with the debut of ESPN in 1979, channels devoted solely to the coverage of sports sprang up across the television landscape with coverage that reached the brink of saturation.

The advent of *USA Today* also contributed to the growing sports media consciousness. With its comprehensive sports page, "McPaper" quickly became a favorite among sports enthusiasts. Readers devoured the national newspaper's "news and notes" section that offered consumers previously unavailable tidbits from across the country.

The exhaustive coverage, be it cable, all-sports radio, Internet, or newsprint, resulted in dozens of voices clamoring to be heard above the din. To stand out among their peers, some reporters occasionally went to extremes when commenting on their beats, resulting in worsening relations between players and the Fourth Estate.

"The game has changed since the time I first knew it, when I was watching my dad and Willie playing, and even later, when I saw Reggie," Bonds lamented. "It seems people used to love the game and love the players. Now, there just seems to be such a negative attitude. I think we've let people get too close to us, and everybody seems to focus on the flaws, the negativism, instead of just enjoying the game."[31]

Indeed, the game had changed drastically since the day of the Say Hey Kid. The lengthy strike of 1994 marked the eighth work stoppage of major league baseball since 1972. As with each previous labor disagreement, the sporting public cared little about the issues involved; they only wanted the differences resolved promptly. On each ensuing occasion a growing portion of the game's fans vowed not to come back to the ball yards when the game resumed. Following each settlement, though, fans returned to the park, even after the prolonged dispute in '81. The 1994 strike, however, would test the patience of even the most diehard fanatic.

Approximately half the owners' revenue was generated from fan attendance. With peak attendance naturally coming during the pennant races of August and September, the Player's Association timed their strike to place the greatest economic stress on the clubs. The strike, which began on August 12, erased the last 52 games of the regular season, and *all* the post-season games. The World Series, which continued even in the depths of the Great Depression, and carried on during two World Wars, was cancelled by the latest disagreement between labor and management.

The longest work stoppage in the history of professional sports didn't end until April 2, 1995, after 234 days. Though the two sides had agreed to play ball again, a new labor agreement wasn't forthcoming in the settlement. A finalized accord was not reached between the warring parties until the fall of '96. A salary cap, the issue which prompted the strike in the first place, was not included in the agreement. Instead, the owners independently developed a revenue-sharing plan that distributed local revenue more equitably. The most notable aspect of the new agreement was the inclusion of a "salary tax" which would be imposed on the five biggest payrolls. Ideally, under a complex formula, the richest franchises would share their local revenue with the less fortunate clubs. However, the protracted ordeal did little to level the economic playing field among the franchises. Player salaries continued to escalate, while the discrepancies between the "haves" and the "have-nots" expanded.

As with each previous work stoppage, the bulk of the public blame was laid at the feet of the Player's Association and its constituents. Fans had little sympathy for any complaints that "overpaid" players might have.

"Unfortunately, the players don't have the P.R. machine the owners have and consequently some of the most talented athletes in the world, at least in the United States, are portrayed as spoiled, rich little brats," Curt Flood explained. "Look, the players are the only resource in this industry, they deserve to be well paid. But the fans believe everything that's delivered to them by the media. Barry Bonds's salary is Barry Bonds's fault. It's what the market has determined."[32]

Lacking the Necessities

On opening day in 1987, major league baseball celebrated the fortieth anniversary of Jackie Robinson's debut with the Brooklyn Dodgers. As the game entered the '87 season, a full 25 percent of the players in the big leagues were either Black or Hispanic. Still, amazingly, forty years after the emergence of Robinson and Larry Doby, the major leagues did not have a single minority manager or general manger. Professional baseball's disgraceful hiring practices for front office openings extended to the minor leagues, where only nine teams out of one hundred and fifty four employed minority managers.

On April 6 Los Angeles Dodgers vice-president Al Campanis appeared on ABC television's *Nightline*, ostensibly to commemorate Jackie Robinson. However, it was *Nightline* host Ted Koppel's inquiry concerning baseball's dismal hiring practices that drew national attention to the show.

"Why is it there are no Black managers, no Black general managers, no Black owners?" Koppel asked the Dodgers executive.

"Well," Campanis answered, "there have been some Black managers, but I really can't answer that question directly."

"Is there still that much prejudice in baseball?" Koppel questioned.

"No, I don't believe it's prejudice," Campanis replied. "I truly believe that they may not have some of the necessities to be, let's say, a field manager, or perhaps a general manager.... How many quarterbacks do you have? How many pitchers do you have that are Black? Why are Black men, or Black people, not good swimmers? Because they don't have the buoyancy."[33]

Campanis's ignorant statements understandably dominated the news in the ensuing days. The encompassing attention cast a pall over the game. The public was surprised to learn, through the *Nightline* interview, the bigoted belief system of high-ranking baseball officials. However, Black men who played the game weren't taken aback by Campanis's statement: Baseball's reluctance to hire minorities for positions of power was not new. Campanis, though, verbalized the bias that remained inherent in the game's hierarchy.

In the aftermath of the *Nightline* fiasco, baseball's minority hiring practices remained a hot topic. Commissioner Peter Ueberroth gave lip service to a plan that supposedly would open minority access to front office positions. Ueberroth's agenda, however, was weak and unimaginative. For a change to actually be implemented, the prejudice that existed in the ranks of upper-level management needed to be addressed.

Some eight months after the Campanis incident, no progress had yet been made. A dozen manager and general-manger positions had come open, but minorities filled none of them.

In Cincinnati, Reds owner Marge Schott believed the controversy didn't involve her. "I'm the only owner who can hug the players," she said. "I feel as close to Eric Davis as to Tracy Jones."[34]

But Schott insisted she would not adhere to Ueberroth's affirmative action plan.

"I would never do anything falsely," she said. "I don't want a token."[35]

Several years later Mrs. Schott made Campanis-like headlines when knowledge of her bigoted nature became public. In two separate instances Schott was reported to have referred to her players in a derogatory manner. Schott, speaking of Eric Davis and Dave Parker, called them her "million dollar niggers," and referred to Reds left fielder Kal Daniels as a "dumb lazy nigger."[36]

As he had in 1987, activist Jesse Jackson stepped forward with a plan that would improve baseball's hiring practices. Jackson offered a ten-point plan for affirmative action. As in '87, Reverend Jackson's proposal lacked depth. His plan set a timetable for the game to reach certain goals in management hiring, but did not include a way to secure the acquiescence of baseball ownership. Instead of implementing Jackson's proposal, major-league baseball offered its own seven-point "minority initiative." Jackson viewed baseball's plan as unacceptable and vowed to organize "a campaign of direct action,"[37] which he implied would include protests at big-league parks.

Through all the controversy, the silence from active players was deafening. Players who didn't hesitate to speak out on issues that concerned their wallet or treatment in the press refused to step forward. "The same courage you see on the field,' said Jackson, "is the opposite of what you see off the field."[38]

"I don't think an issue like that should be talked about every day,"

New York Yankee Danny Tartabull said. "Why sit there and pummel somebody every day with an issue?"[39]

"It's not my place to fight it," Barry Bonds contended. "That's why we have a Jesse Jackson. I don't agree with discrimination or racism, but I'm not in the front office. I'm on the front line. I'm a Black athlete who has been well taken care of."[40]

Thanks to the apathy of top minority stars like Tartabull and Bonds, progress was minimal. Bonds apparently was never taught the old adage, "Strike while the iron is hot." If he had been he would have understood that the best time to protest the politics of the game was while he was among the elite in his profession. When he is no longer on "the front lines," Barry will learn, like many men of his father's era, that the game has little use for him and his peers.

Following the Schott public-relations flap, a handful of minorities were given the opportunity to manage in the big leagues. In nearly every instance, success followed the novice field generals. Cito Gaston, Dusty Baker, Don Baylor and Felipe Alou all proved to be among the game's finest managers. In 1993, six minorities held major-league managerial positions, a high point that would not be approached again after Tony Perez was fired just forty-four games into the season. "Managers," it has been said, "are hired to be fired," and for years an old-boys' network has seen to it that managers don't stay out of work for long. Black managers, however, rarely received a second opportunity once they are dismissed. Over the course of the next few years, Gaston, Hal McRae and Don Baylor all followed Perez onto the scrap heap of unemployed managers.

There were twenty major league managerial changes between 1995 and the fall of 1996; a white applicant filled every opening. With the pressure of the Campanis and Schott episodes dissipated, baseball executives reverted to their natural inclinations.

Again in 1999, though, baseball found itself making empty promises. This time the promises came from the mouth of Bud Selig, the current commissioner of baseball. Selig ordered the game's owners to consider minority candidates when openings became available in five categories, including general manager and manager.

"If a club has an opening in any of these positions, the club owner must notify me personally," the commissioner wrote in a letter to owners. "In addition your list of candidates must be provided to me. I expect the list to include minority candidates whom you and your staff have identified. I will provide assistance to you if you cannot identify candidates on your own."[41]

To impress upon the owners how serious he was about this most unusual directive, Selig added an unveiled threat. "I will not be reluctant to impose sanctions on clubs that do not comply,"[42] he wrote.

Still, even in light of the memo, Selig insisted to reporters that "significant" progress had been made in recent years in minority hiring. The commissioner apparently was not privy to some vital statistics. From the first day of 1993 until the spring of 1999, only one minority manager, Jerry Manuel of the Chicago White Sox, had been hired. In addition, the game's first Black general manager, Bob Watson, won a World Series with the Yankees only to be out of a job within weeks..

Following the 2000 season, six managerial positions opened. Frank Robinson, working out of major-league baseball's offices under the title of "Baseball's vice-president for on-field operations," offered high expectations for the forthcoming hiring. "There are six jobs out there," he said. "Anything less than fifty percent (minority hiring) would be another failure on the part of baseball."[43]

Unsurprisingly, baseball did not live up to Robinson's high standard. Under the pressure of another Bud Selig directive, which demanded that each team in search of a manger interview at least one minority candidate (interviews that the commissioner expected to be "sincere"), a virtual parade of well-publicized interviews with minority applicants took place. As the dust cleared and the charade ended, only one minority manager was hired: Lloyd McClendon of the Pittsburgh Pirates.

One general manager in search of a field manager, Gord Ash of Toronto, admitted, "Minority hiring has to be a front-of-mind position, because too often our circle of acquaintances does not include minorities." Ash, who, like the game's other twenty-nine general mangers, is white, went on, "If you do not work in a pro-active position in the organization, it's not going to happen."[44] Ash then proceeded to fill Toronto's opening with a white candidate with no previous managerial experience, Buck Martinez.

"The only way we can make baseball executives understand that we are qualified is to demand that we be given the chance to prove we can lead as well as follow," Jackie Robinson wrote in 1964.

With words that still rang true three and a half decades after he put them to paper, Robinson continued. "To make baseball stronger, to make the country stronger, the talent and skills of every American, regardless of color, should be used. Baseball was never truly an all-American game until we got into it. This will never be a truly American country until we can compete everywhere on equal terms."[45]

Why Isn't Barry Bonds Willie Mays?

For the most part, Barry's early problems with the press could be attributed to his resentment of the treatment handed his father when Bobby was an active player. Some of the negative press the elder Bonds received could be attributed to the color of his skin, a not unusual case during the decade of the seventies. Because of his own personal actions, though, Barry couldn't pin the blame for his poor press relations on his Blackness. Instead, Barry's difficulties with the media were self-inflicted. With his arrogance and condescending manner, Bonds alienated practically every media person he encountered.

On the other hand, when the mood came over him, Barry could be a most pleasant interview subject. Indignant one moment, charming the next, Bonds had proved himself to be a complex subject.

"Barry Bonds can be rude and intimidating," Carrie Muskat wrote in *Baseball Weekly,* "or he can flash a million dollar smile and thoughtfully answer questions in a gentle, soft spoken manner — if you wait until he's ready. You've got to play by his rules."[46]

Muskat recognized a fact that many of her colleagues either missed or chose to ignore; Bonds could be approachable ... on his own terms.

As his career evolved, Barry recognized a need to rehabilitate his public persona. Through the first half of the nineties most experts conceded that Bonds was the best player in the game. Yet few superstars were held in lower esteem. Several pieces appeared in print waxing nostalgic, pining for a more innocent era, when sports heroes could be admired. Without fail, Bonds's name appeared as the antithesis of baseball's golden age idols.

"Why Isn't Barry Bonds Willie Mays?" a *Gentleman's Quarterly* article asked.

"So. To begin with," Peter Richmond surmised, "in Barry Bonds' defense — in defense of Willie Mays' godson — it used to be easier to be a hero.

"When the godfather played the game, there were communities for whom baseball was a singular sport and a singular thing. And there were athletes who counted themselves members of the community."[47]

The days when an active superstar would join the neighborhood children in a game of stickball had long since passed. The opportunities presented for the millionaire ballplayer to become a part of the local community were far less romantic, but almost certainly more constructive. With growing frequency, modern athletes used charitable outlets as a means of integrating themselves into the fabric of their community.

Possibly, Barry was more active than most of his contemporaries when it came to donating his time and name to charitable causes. Immediately upon moving to San Francisco, Barry's altruism came to the fore. Bonds endorsed a number of Bay Area community services including a blood drive at Alameda–Contra Costa County blood bank, and also registering with, and promoting, the National Marrow Donor Program. Barry also supported Adopt a Special Kid Foundation and was a member of the board of directors of the United Way.

His good work did much to rehabilitate his image on a local level, but nationally Barry was still viewed as a villain. As his career approached its closing stages, though, Bonds finally began to take responsibility for much of his public image.

"Listen," he said, "I know a lot of what happened to me in my career is my fault. I understand that I shouldn't have rebelled the way I did early in my career. Maybe I spent too much time worrying about how I was going to live up to what my dad had done playing, and what my godfather had done.

"Had I handled the media like Michael (Jordan) and Magic (Johnson), things may have turned out different. I should have taken things more humorously. But I was always focused on people calling me Bobby instead of Barry.

"I love baseball, but I don't like the politics of the game. The game has changed since the time I first knew it.... It seems people used to love the game and love the players. Now, there just seems to be such a negative attitude. I think we've let people get too close to us, and everybody seems to focus on the flaws, the negativity, instead of just enjoying the game."[48]

The purity that Bonds wistfully recalled had long ago vanished from the game. Expansion, free agency, labor unrest, drug abuse, and an overzealous press, all added to the diminishing appeal of the National Pastime. The sporting public had also wearied of the cantankerous, overpaid and unappreciative players who seemed to dominate the headlines of their morning papers.

" I sell papers," Bonds once said, "I sell papers better than anybody in baseball."[49] And he was correct. Barry's position as baseball's best player and the game's most unpredictable quote made it so. The public, against its better judgment, continued to buy what Bonds, his contemporaries and the sporting press pandered.

In the second inning of San Francisco's August 23, 1998 game against the Florida Marlins, Bonds hit a home run against Kirk Ojala. The blast was the 400th of Barry's career. Paired with his 438 stolen bases, it made Bonds the first 400/400 player in the history of the game.

"I'd like to get 500/500," Bonds confided after his monumental achievement. "I think 600 would be too hard. I wouldn't want to keep going just to get those numbers, if I thought I was hurting the team."[50]

"I want to be remembered as the best left fielder ever to play baseball. All the other positions are taken. But no one talks about the greatest left fielder, a guy who dominated that one position."[51]

In addition to his unprecedented offensive numbers, Bonds had accumulated eight Gold Gloves through the 1999 season. Only one aspect of Barry's baseball resumé remained lacking: a successful conclusion to the post-season. However, even without a championship ring on his finger, Bonds had proven to be a most worthy heir to his father's and godfather's legacies. In the latter stage of his often turbulent career, Barry had found peace with himself, if not with a recalcitrant press corps.

"I'll tell you something," he said in an *Esquire* magazine interview, " at this stage in my life, in my career, I'm more comfortable with myself than I've ever been. I'm a very happy person, except maybe when I'm in a slump.... I know the truth about myself."[52]

"I've been playing against ghosts all my life," Barry said. "I'm playing against a godfather, Mr. October, and my own father. And I'm stuck in the middle of what baseball wants and who they are. I'm never going to be who they are. But people want me to be as great or greater. But I can only be as good as I want to be. And as I'm capable of being."[53]

Summer of '73

While the San Francisco Giants were preparing for the 2001 season, ESPN sent a reporter to question Bonds.

The fact that Barry would one day enter the Baseball Hall of Fame was a foregone conclusion as Bonds readied himself for his 16th major league campaign. What was he going to *say* when standing on the dais in Cooperstown on his Induction Day, was the question posed by ESPN's interviewer.

Looking straight into the camera, Bonds simply responded, "Thank you, but you missed the show."[54]

Barry was coming off another typically excellent year. With 49 home runs, a .306 batting average and 106 runs batted in, Bonds led the Giants to a playoff birth and once again found himself in the running for league MVP.

Reminiscent of 1991, Bonds finished second in the balloting. On this occasion he was bested by teammate Jeff Kent. Unlike in '91, Barry's runner-up status wasn't viewed as an oversight; even Giant manager Dusty

Barry Bonds in 2001 on the way to home run number 73 (© Duomo/CORBIS).

Baker endorsed Kent for the award. Baker's honesty derailed any chance Bonds might have had to capture an unprecedented fourth MVP.

Running second to Kent may have disappointed Bonds, but his failure once again to produce in the post-season was a bigger frustration. Against the New York Mets in the division playoffs, Bonds batted only .176 with just one RBI. The lack of productivity in the playoffs remained the only blemish on Barry's sterling career.

Barry's career high 49 home runs in 2000 in no way prepared the sporting public for what was to come. The possibility of 71 in 2001 entered the minds of baseball enthusiasts as early as the beginning of June. Though Bonds began the season 0–21 at the bat, his slump was short-lived. Barry's bat was afire in short order, letting loose unprecedented barrage of home runs. The national media took notice of Barry's scintillating home-run pace, and began to pepper Bonds with interview requests. Not surprisingly, Barry did not relish the interaction with his adversaries in the press.

"It's straining to talk about it," Bonds said, referring to his rapid home-run rate. "We're trying to win games here. It's not a home run hitting contest. We're trying to get to the World Series."[55]

Bonds was in a precarious position. Talk about his home runs and he would be perceived as self-centered. Deflect the discussion from himself and focus on team goals, and Barry would be seen as "uncooperative."

Years of bad press had come home to roost. Barry tried to continue the rehabilitation of his public persona, an attempt that received wide publicity but was met with great skepticism in the media.

"Bonds personified the introverted, complex, intelligent, crowd shunning, media-disdaining kind of loner — obsessed with himself and his craft, but oblivious even to his own teammates— who scare the daylights out of any sport,"[56] wrote Thomas Boswell of the *Washington Post*.

Barry's attempted rehabilitation only went so far. Perhaps the most damning piece yet written on Bonds was published in the midst of Barry's quest for the single-season home-run record.

In the August 27, 2001, issue of *Sports Illustrated*, columnist Rick Reily ripped into Bonds for nearly every offense imaginable, allowing only that Barry is a "brilliant" player.

"In the San Francisco Giants' clubhouse, everybody knows the score: 24–1," Reily penned. "There are 24 teammates, and there's Barry Bonds."

"Bonds isn't beloved by his teammates. He's not even beliked. He often doesn't run out grounders, doesn't run out flies... He's an MTV diva, only with bigger earring."[57]

Reily seemingly relished lashing out in print at Bonds's personality shortcomings.

"Someday they'll be able to hold Bonds' funeral in a fitting room,"[58] he wrote.

Reily went to Jeff Kent in the hope of exploiting Barry's lack of popularity in the Giant clubhouse. "On the field, we're fine," Kent told the reporter, "but off the field, I don't care about Barry and Barry doesn't care about me ... or anybody else."[59] Reily's column fulfilled its purpose. The anti–Bonds rhetoric served as fodder for sports talk radio for weeks, further fueling a negative sentiment towards Barry that already existed in the public's mind.

Much of the discussion throughout the summer centered not on Bonds' chances of breaking Mark McGwire's record, but, rather, on whether he *deserved* to hold the exalted mark. Some dismissed his run toward 71. "He's not a 'power hitter' per se," was one argument, and these critics pointed to Barry's previous best output of 49.

Indeed, despite his deluge of home runs, the public was more ambivalent than energized. Compared with the summer of 1998, when McGwire and Sammy Sosa "saved" the game with their assault on Roger Maris's vaunted record of 61, Barry's record-breaking campaign was met with a curious indifference.

Debate was abundant examining the lack of interest in Bonds's chase. Was it his personality? Was it the fact that McGwire's mark of 70 was only three years old? Perhaps, some ventured, it was the color of Barry's skin that kept a segment of the public's interest to a minimum? Conceivably, a germ of truth lay in each presumption.

Even the venerated Mark McGwire minimized Barry's run for his record. "As far as media coverage and scrutiny, there is no way that what he's going through is even close to what I tried to go through."[60]

It is certainly true that the media crush was much greater in '97 as

McGwire chased Roger Maris's thirty-seven-year-old record. McGwire conveniently forgot that the great majority of the sporting public was backing his pursuit. Undeniably the media crush on McGwire's time was relentless and at times crossed the line and became an invasion of his privacy. Nevertheless, to diminish Bonds's experience smacked of envy.

The September 11 attacks on America further diminished the significance of the home run mark. The press covered Bonds with reluctance, but nonetheless with great thoroughness. When the moment finally came, only 15,000 fans remained at Pac Bell Park. The majority of the sold-out crowd had left prior to the conclusion of the longest nine-inning game in baseball history (4 hour, 27 minutes), and was not present when Bonds was honored following the Giants' 11–10 loss on October 5th (and 6th) to the Dodgers. Even in his greatest moment of personal glory, Bonds's achievement was overshadowed by his team's elimination from the pennant race. Home runs number 71 and 72 placed Barry Bonds in the pantheon of baseball's immortals.

Bonds addressed the crowd in a post-game ceremony.

"We've come a long way. We've had our ups and downs," Barry said as his emotions threatened to overwhelm him, "Thank you."[61]

Just as Bowie Kuhn was not present when Henry Aaron passed Babe Ruth as the all-time home-run champ, Bud Selig was absent from Bonds's achievement. The commissioner was in Houston, where he extolled Barry's great feat. "What Barry has done is a remarkable accomplishment. He has demonstrated on a national stage why he is one of the greatest players of our generation" *San Francisco Examiner* 10-6-2001.

Selig's failure to be present in San Francisco was a microcosm of the public's indifferent reception to Bond's record-breaking season. At the close of the season Barry had 567 lifetime home runs, having passed ten different Hall of Famers on the all-time list through the course of the season, and within reach of Aaron's mark of 755.

In addition to the single-season home-run record, Barry set new standards for most walks in a season with 177, and finished with a .863 slugging percentage, a full 16 points better than the previous record. The culmination of Bonds's effort was, unfortunately, not an appearance in the World Series. Rather, Barry was once again saluted for individual excellence when he was named the National League's Most Valuable Player for an unprecedented fourth time.

Though he was thirty-seven years old, Bonds refused to concede anything to age ... or his critics. "I'm like Ali," Barry declared. "I'm going to keep on ticking. Y'all are not going to run me out of this game yet."[62]

7

We Need to Do Better

Jackie Robinson ended his autobiography with a statement to which many of his African American contemporaries could relate. "There is one irrefutable fact of my life, which has determined much of what happened to me. I was a Black man in a white world. *I never had it made.*"[1]

Though the integration of baseball opened new doors of opportunity for Blacks, it prefigured the demise of economic independence enjoyed by Blacks in the Negro Leagues. Jackie Robinson's arrival, while offering new possibilities in "organized" baseball, effectively spelled the end of the all-Black leagues, and thus killed Black enterprise in the game. The Negro Leagues that were once ruled by a Black president, officiated by Black umpires, managed by Black field managers and assembled by Black owners had vanished.

Blacks have been welcomed to the major leagues largely as paid performers only. The number of Black umpires in the major leagues can be counted on one hand. Front office and managerial positions have been continually contracted on the basis of amity and not competence. Furthermore, with the dawn of the twenty-first century major league baseball has yet to have a Black owner. The most prominent title thus far held by an African American, the National League presidency, is largely a ceremonial position.

During the 2001 World Series, Bud Selig addressed inquiries concerning baseball's minority hiring practices. Despite obvious shortcomings, the commissioner told reporters that he was content with the progress made under his leadership. "Whenever the next meeting is … it's a subject I want to talk to all the clubs about," Selig said. "I don't have any criticism at this point. Everyone has followed my memorandum. But we need to do better."[2]

Selig's determination to "do better" did little to reassure many around the profession. Less than two weeks after the Arizona Diamondbacks defeated the New York Yankees for the '01 world championship, the game's inequitable employment practices were once again the subject of headlines.

Former major-league pitcher Dave Stewart, who had worked as an assistant general manager with the Toronto Blue Jays, alleged that baseball owners had a bias when hiring for prominent front-office positions.

"They think the only people capable of doing these jobs are white people, not minorities," Stewart said after being passed over for the position of general manager in Toronto.

"I'm not speaking just for me, I'm speaking for a lot of minority candidates who have not been given the opportunity," Stewart clarified. "The system doesn't work. The playing field is never going to be equal. The man I work for here [with the Blue Jays], Paul Godfrey, told me he would like me to take on his manager's job before he hired Buck Martinez."

"Why is it OK to hire me to manage his club, but not OK for me to be his general manager? It's just little messages. I made it perfectly clear this is the direction I wanted to be in. It's just little signs that it's perfectly acceptable for me to be on the field, but there's discomfort with me being in front-office management."[3]

Others disagreed with Stewart's assessment. Speaking at a January 11, 2002, luncheon, former major-league manager Whitey Herzog contended that baseball was guilty of "reverse" discrimination. Herzog was the keynote speaker at the annual Iowa Cubs FanFest.

"I do think that there's a lot of capable minorities," Herzog said. "But I do think today, the people that are really getting it stuck to them are guys like this guy over here because he isn't a minority" *Herzog: Reverse Discrimination Exists in Baseball* 1-12-2002 Miller, Bryce, *DesMoines Register.*

Herzog was referring to Iowa manager Bruce Kimm, who is white.

Some would argue that the best evidence that baseball has progressed on the racial front is the claim of "reverse" discrimination. The numbers, however, simply do not back up these allegations. Qualified minorities are continually overlooked for managerial and general manager posts, while their white counterparts, even men with little experience, fill the vacant positions.

Since the commissioner's office holds no power that would allow Selig to command a team to hire anyone, regardless of race, his 1999 dictate was little more than window dressing. Yes, clubs began to include more minorities in the interviewing process; however, to many the whole process reeked of tokenism.

Chris Chambliss was one of the usual suspects marched out every year. Eminently qualified, Chambliss is nevertheless overlooked each and every year. When asked if he believed race played a part in his being passed over, Chambliss replied with the diplomacy of a man still hoping to someday catch on as a big-league manager.

"We can only speculate," Chambliss said. "Why haven't I managed? I don't really know. I've been interviewing every year. I'm proud that people think I'm able to manage and I've gotten the interviews."

He then added, "Maybe its not my time yet."[4]

Curt Flood died of throat cancer on January 20, 1997, at the age of 59. Flood's lasting impact on the game of baseball was commemorated, and his courage eulogized. No tribute, though, was more noteworthy than the statement issued by President Bill Clinton on October 27, 1998. On that fall day Clinton introduced the "Curt Flood Act of 1998."

"It is especially fitting that this legislation honors a courageous baseball player and individual; the late Curt Flood, whose enormous talents on the baseball diamond were matched by his courage off the field,"[5] Clinton said.

The newly created legislation limited the antitrust exemption previously granted baseball.

"[Flood's] stand set in motion the events that culminate in the bill I have signed into law," Clinton explained. "It is sound policy to treat the employment matters of Major League Baseball players under the antitrust laws in the same way such matters are treated for athletes in other professional sports."[6]

Flood's good friend and Cardinal teammate Lou Brock acknowledged the obvious relationship between Curt and Jackie Robinson. "Although they're parallel, one has to do with a social issue of tolerance levels, and the other has to do with a dynamic economic change," Brock said. "Jackie Robinson impacted the world in terms of race relations. What Curt did is change the relationship of how people do business with each other, regardless of race. The world took notice of both."[7]

Flood and Robinson fulfilled the promise fostered by their forebears: the promise inherent in the democratic ideals underlying American culture; equal opportunity for every man … a chance to prove one's worth on a level playing field.

Notes

Chapter 1

1. A.S. "Doc" Young, "Rube Foster: Baseball's Negro Pioneer," *Hue Magazine* August 1957.
2. Frank A. Young, "Rube Foster: The Mastermind of Baseball," *Abbott's Monthly* November 1930.
3. Robert Peterson, *Only the Ball Was White: A History of the Legendary Black Players and All-Black Teams,* 1994.
4. Al Monroe, "What Is the Matter with Baseball?" April 1932.
5. R. Peterson, *Only the Ball Was White.*
6. Frank A. Young, "Rube Foster: The Mastermind of Baseball."
7. Frank A. Young, "Rube Foster: The Mastermind of Baseball."
8. Frank A. Young, "Rube Foster: The Mastermind of Baseball."
9. A.S. Young, "Rube Foster: Baseball's Negro Pioneer."
10. Sol White, *Sol White's History of Colored Baseball,* 1995.
11. A.S. Young, "Rube Foster: Baseball's Negro Pioneer."
12. Jerry Malloy, "Rube Foster and Black Baseball in Chicago."
13. Malloy, "Rube Foster and Black Baseball in Chicago."
14. John Holway, *Blackball Stars: Negro League Pioneers,* 1988.
15. Holway, *Blackball Stars.*
16. Holway, *Blackball Stars.*
17. Bob Peterson, "Rube Foster, Best of the Black Managers," May, 1975.
18. Frank A. Young, "Rube Foster: The Mastermind of Baseball."
19. Frank A. Young, "Rube Foster: The Mastermind of Baseball."
20. Holway, *Blackball Stars.*
21. Bob Peterson, "Rube Foster, Best of the Black Managers."
22. Malloy, "Black Baseball In Chicago.
23. Adrian C Anson, *Ball Player's Career*, 1900.
24. David W. Zang, *Fleet Walker's Divided Heart: The Life of Baseball's First Black Major Leaguer*, 1995.
25. Mark Ribowsky, *A Complete History of the Negro Leagues 1884–1955*, 1995.
26. Holway, *Blackball Stars.*
27. Phil Dixon, with P.J. Hannigan, *The Negro Baseball Leagues, 1867–1955: A Photographic History*, 1992.
28. Frank A. Young, "Rube Foster: The Mastermind of Baseball."
29. Malloy, "Rube Foster and Black Baseball in Chicago."
30. Monroe, "What Is the Matter with Baseball?".
31. Frank A. Young, "Rube Foster: The Mastermind of Baseball."
32. Monroe, "What Is the Matter with Baseball?"
33. Malloy, "Rube Foster and Black Baseball in Chicago."

34. Ribowsky, *A Complete History of the Negro Leagues 1884-1955*, Mark Birch Lane Press, 1995.

35. Monroe, "What Is the Matter with Baseball?"

36. *The Sporting News*, August 8, 1981.

37. R. Peterson, *Only the Ball Was White*.

38. *The Sporting News*, August 8, 1981.

39. Rollo Wilson, *The Pittsburgh Courier*, December 1930.

40. *Chicago Defender*, December 12, 1930.

41. A.S. Young, "Rube Foster: Baseball's Negro Pioneer."

42. Malloy, "Rube Foster and Black Baseball in Chicago."

Chapter 2

1. LeRoy (Satchel) Paige, *Pitchin' Man: Satchel Paige's Own Story*, as told to Hal Lebovitz, 1992.

2. Paige as told to Lebovitz, *Pitchin' Man*.

3. Paige as told to Lebovitz, *Pitchin' Man*.

4. Paige as told to Lebovitz, *Pitchin' Man*.

5. Paige as told to Lebovitz, *Pitchin' Man*.

6. Paige as told to Lebovitz, *Pitchin' Man*.

7. Paige as told to Lebovitz, *Pitchin' Man*.

8. Paige as told to Lebovitz, *Pitchin' Man*.

9. Paige as told to Lebovitz, *Pitchin' Man*.

10. Paige as told to Lebovitz, *Pitchin' Man*.

11. Paige as told to Lebovitz, *Pitchin' Man*.

12. Rob Ruck, *Kings of the Hill: Baseball's Forgotten Men* (Video), 1993.

13. John Holway, *Voices from the Great Black Baseball Leagues*, 1992.

14. LeRoy (Satchel) Paige as told to David Lipman, *Maybe I'll Pitch Forever: The Hilarious Story Behind the Legend*, 1962.

15. *The Pittsburgh Courier*, May 6, 1944.

16. Paige as told to Lipman, *Maybe I'll Pitch Forever*.

17. Paige as told to Lipman, *Maybe I'll Pitch Forever*.

18. Paige as told to Lipman, *Maybe I'll Pitch Forever*.

19. Paige as told to Lebovitz, *Pitchin' Man*.

20. Paige as told to Lipman, *Maybe I'll Pitch Forever*.

21. Paige as told to Lipman, *Maybe I'll Pitch Forever*.

22. Richard Donovan, "The Fabulous Satchel Paige," *Collier's*, May 10–June 13, 1953.

23. Paige as told to Lebovitz, *Pitchin' Man*.

24. Jim Bankes, *The Pittsburgh Crawfords: The Life and Times of Black Baseball's Most Exciting Team*, 1991.

25. Bankes, *The Pittsburgh Crawfords*.

26. Bankes, *The Pittsburgh Crawfords*.

27. Bankes, *The Pittsburgh Crawfords*.

28. Bankes, *The Pittsburgh Crawfords*.

29. Robert Gregory, *Diz: Dizzy Dean and Baseball During the Great Depression*, 1992.

30. Bill Veeck with Ed Linn, *Veeck as in Wreck: The Autobiography of Bill Veeck*, 1962.

31. Mark Ribowsky, *Don't Look Back: Satchel Paige in the Shadow of Baseball*, 1994.

32. Jules Tygiel, *Baseball's Great Experiment: Jackie Robinson and His Legacy*, 1983.

33. Mark Ribowsky, *Don't Look Back*.

34. Janet Bruce, *The Kansas City Monarchs: Champions of Black Baseball*, 1985.

35. John Holway, *Black Ball Stars: Negro League Pioneers*, 1988.

36. Tygiel, *Baseball's Great Experiment*.

37. Paige as told to Lebovitz, *Pitchin' Man*.

38. Paige as told to Lipman, *Maybe I'll Pitch Forever.*
39. Tygiel, *Baseball's Great Experiment.*
40. Tygiel, *Baseball's Great Experiment.*
41. Mark Ribowky, *A Complete History of the Negro Leagues, 1884-1955*, 1995.
42. Murray Polner, *Branch Rickey: A Biography*, 1982.
43. Tygiel, *Baseball's Great Experiment.*
44. Donovan, "The Fabulous Satchel Paige."
45. Veeck with Linn, *Veeck as in Wreck.*
46. Veeck with Linn, *Veeck as in Wreck.*
47. Donovan, "The Fabulous Satchel Paige."
48. Donovan, "The Fabulous Satchel Paige."
49. Donovan, "The Fabulous Satchel Paige."
50. Donovan, "The Fabulous Satchel Paige."
51. *The Sporting News*, August 8, 1948.
52. Paige as told to Lipman, *Maybe I'll Pitch Forever.*
53. Paige as told to Lebovitz, *Pitchin' Man.*
54. Donovan, "The Fabulous Satchel Paige."
55. Paige as told to Lebovitz, *Pitchin' Man.*
56. *Pittsburgh Courier*, October 16, 1948.
57. Veeck with Linn, *Veeck as in Wreck.*
58. Ribowsky, *Don't Look* .
59. Paige as told to Lebovitz, *Pitchin' Man.*
60. Paige as told to Lipman, *Maybe I'll Pitch Forever.*
61. Paige as told to Lipman, *Maybe I'll Pitch Forever.*
62. Donovan, "The Fabulous Satchel Paige."
63. Donovan, "The Fabulous Satchel Paige."
64. Paige as told to Lebovitz, *Pitchin' Man.*
65. *Saturday Evening Post*, July 27, 1940.
66. George DeGregorio, *Joe DiMaggio: An Informal Biography*, 1981.
67. Paige as told to Lebovitz, *Pitchin' Man.*
68. Veeck with Linn, *Veeck as in Wreck.*
69. Paige as told to Lipman, *Maybe I'll Pitch Forever.*
70. Paige as told to Lipman, *Maybe I'll Pitch Forever.*
71. Paige as told to Lipman, *Maybe I'll Pitch Forever.*

Chapter 3

1. Jules Tygiel, *Baseball's Great Experiment: Jackie Robinson and His Legacy.*
2. Bill Koening. "As the First Black Player, Larry Doby Endured No Less a Burden," July 2, 1997.
3. Joseph Thomas Moore, *Pride Against Prejudice*, 1988.
4. Moore, *Pride Against Prejudice.*
5. *New Jersey Afro-American*, June 20, 1942.
6. Moore, *Pride Against Prejudice.*
7. Red Barber, *1947: When All Hell Broke Loose in Baseball*, 1982.
8. Bill Veeck with Ed Linn, *Veeck as in Wreck: The Autobiography of Bill Veeck*, 1962.
9. Tygiel, *Baseball's Great Experiment.*
10. Tygiel, *Baseball's Great Experiment.*
11. John Holway, *Voices from the Great Black Baseball Leagues*, 1992.
12. Veeck with Linn, *Veeck as in Wreck.*
13. Moore, *Pride Against Prejudice.*
14. Moore, *Pride Against Prejudice.*
15. Koening, "As the First Black Player, Larry Doby Endured No Less a Burden."
16. Tygiel, *Baseball's Great Experiment.*
17. Veeck with Linn, *Veeck as in Wreck.*
18. Veeck with Linn, *Veeck as in Wreck.*
19. Veeck with Linn, *Veeck as in Wreck.*

20. Koening, "As the First Black Player, Larry Doby Endured No Less a Burden."
21. Moore, *Pride Against Prejudice.*
22. Veeck with Linn, *Veeck as in Wreck.*
23. Moore, *Pride Against Prejudice.*
24. Terry Egan, "Similar, But Not the Same, Larry Doby Was a Lesser-Known Pioneer" *Dallas Morning News*, April 4, 1997.
25. Moore, *Pride Against Prejudice.*
26. "Robinson Opened the Doors for Many But Not Doby," *Washington Post*, July 9, 1997.
27. *Call and Post*, July 12, 1947
28. Moore, *Pride Against Prejudice.*
29. Moore, *Pride Against Prejudice.*
30. Veeck with Linn, *Veeck As in Wreck.*
31. "Robinson Opened the Doors for Many But Not Doby," *Washington Post*, July 9, 1997.
32. Veeck with Linn, *Veeck as in Wreck.*
33. Veeck with Linn, *Veeck as in Wreck.*
34. *Cleveland Plain Dealer*, March 3, 1948.
35. Moore, *Pride Against Prejudice.*
36. Moore, *Pride Against Prejudice.*
37. *The Pittsburgh Courier*, October 12, 1948.
38. Moore, *Pride Against Prejudice.*
39. *Cleveland Press*, October 26, 1955.
40. Moore, *Pride Against Prejudice.*
41. Moore, *Pride Against Prejudice.*
42. *Ebony*, September 1957.
43. Moore, *Pride Against Prejudice.*
44. *Washington Post*, June 6, 1957.
45. Moore, *Pride Against Prejudice.*
46. Tygiel, *Baseball's Great Experiment.*
47. Moore, *Pride Against Prejudice.*
48. Tygiel, *Baseball's Great Experiment.*
49. Patrick Harrigan, *The Detroit Tigers: Club and Community*, 1997.
50. Michael Betzhold, *Queen of Diamonds: The Tiger Stadium Story*, 1992.
51. Bruce Kuklick, *To Everything a Season*: Shibe Park and Urban Philadelphia, 1991.
52. Tygiel, *Baseball's Great Experiment.*
53. Tygiel, *Baseball's Great Experiment.*
54. Tygiel, *Baseball's Great Experiment.*
55. Tygiel, *Baseball's Great Experiment.*
56. Tygiel, *Baseball's Great Experiment.*
57. Tygiel, *Baseball's Great Experiment.*
58. Tygiel, *Baseball's Great Experiment.*
59. Tygiel, *Baseball's Great Experiment.*
60. Koening, *Baseball Weekly*- As the First Black Player, Larry Doby Endured No Less a Burden.

Chapter 4

1. Letter from Curt Flood to Bowie Kuhn, December 24, 1969.
2. Curt Flood with Richard Carter, *The Way It Is*, 1971.
3. Flood with Carter, *The Way It Is.*
4. Flood with Carter, *The Way It Is.*
5. Frank Robinson with Barry Stainback, *Extra Innings*, 1988.
6. Flood with Carter, *The Way It Is.*
7. Flood with Carter, *The Way It Is.*
8. Flood with Carter, *The Way It Is.*
9. Flood with Carter, *The Way It Is.*
10. Flood with Carter, *The Way It Is.*
11. Jack R. Robinson, *Baseball Has Done It*, edited by Charles Dexter, 1964.
12. Willie Stargell with Tom Bird, *Stargell: An Autobiography*, 1984.
13. Dick Allen and Tim Whitaker, *Crash: The Life and Times of Dick Allen*, 1989.
14. Allen and Whitaker, *Crash.*
15. Allen and Whitaker, *Crash.*
16. Stargell with Bird, *Stargell.*
17. Robinson. *Baseball Has Done It.*
18. Robinson. *Baseball Has Done It.*
19. Allen and Whitaker, *Crash.*
20. Flood with Carter, *The Way It Is.*
21. *The Sporting News*, March 27, 1971.
22. Bob Gibson with Lonnie Wheeler, *Stranger to the Game*, 1994.
23. Gibson with Wheeler, *Stranger to the Game.*
24. "Not Just a Flood, But a Deluge," *Sports Illustrated*, August 19, 1968.
25. "Not Just a Flood, But a Deluge," *Sports Illustrated*, August 19, 1968.
26. Flood with Carter, *The Way It Is.*
27. *The Sporting News*, March 21, 1971.

28. *The Sporting News,* March 21, 1971.
29. John Heylar, *The Lords of the Realm: The Real History of Baseball,* 1994
30. Flood with Carter, *The Way It Is.*
31. Marvin Miller, *A Whole Different Ball Game,* 1991.
32. John Heylar, *The Lords of the Realm: The Real History of Baseball,* 1994.
33. Flood with Carter, *The Way It Is.*
34. Miller, *A Whole Different Ball Game.*
35. Miller, *A Whole Different Ball Game.*
36. Frederick Douglass, *Narrative of the Life of Frederick Douglass, An American Slave,* 1960.
37. Ken Burns and Gregory C. Ward, *Baseball: An Illustrated History,* 1994.
38. *Brown v Board of Education,* 347 U.S. 483 (1954).
39. Flood with Carter, *The Way It Is.*
40. Bob Gibson with Phil Pepe, *From Ghetto to Glory: The Story of Bob Gibson,* 1970.
41. Robert Boyle, "The Private World of the Negro Ball Player," *Sports Illustrated,* March 21, 1960.
42. Hank Aaron with Lonnie Wheeler, *I Had a Hammer: The Hank Aaron Story,* 1991.
43. Flood with Carter, *The Way It Is.*
44. Malcolm X, *Malcolm X Speaks,* edited by George Brietman, 1965.
45. "Fists for Freedom," HBO documentary, 1999.
46. Arnold Ramperstad, *Jackie Robinson: A Biography,* 1997.
47. Kenneth J. Jennings, *Balls and Strikes: The Money Game in Professional Baseball,* 1990.
48. Letter from Curt Flood to Bowie Kuhn, December 24, 1969.
49. "Curt Flood and the Baseball Revolution," *LA Weekly,* April 7, 1994.
50. Letter from Bowie Kuhn to Curt Flood, December 30, 1969.
51. *New York Daily News,* January 18, 1970.
52. *New York Daily News,* January 18, 1970.
53. Flood with Carter, *The Way It Is,* 1971.
54. *Toolson v N.Y. Yankees,* 346 U.S. 356.
55. *The Sporting News,* June 6, 1970.
56. Flood with Carter, *The Way It Is.*
57. *New York Times,* June 6, 1970.
58. Bill Veeck with Ed Linn, *Veeck as in Wreck,* 1962.
59. Veeck with Linn, *Veeck as in Wreck.*
60. Jim Bouton and Leonard Schecter, *Ball Four: My Life and Hard Times Throwing The Knuckle Ball in the Big Leagues,* 1970.
61. Miller, *A Whole Different Ball Game.*
62. *New York Daily News,* January 18, 1970.
63. *New York Times,* December 19, 1970.
64. *New York Times,* December 19, 1970.
65. *New York Times,* December 19, 1970.
66. *The Sporting News,* April 29, 1971.
67. *The Sporting News,* April 29, 1971.
68. *The Sporting News,* April 29, 1971.
69. *The Sporting News,* June 1, 1972.
70. Martin Luther King, Jr., *A Testament of Hope: The Essential Writings of Martin Luther King, Jr.,* edited by James M. Washington, 1986.
71. Bob Woodward and Scott Armstrong, *The Brethern: Inside the Supreme Court,* 1979.
72. *Flood v Kuhn,* 407 U.S. 258.
73. *Flood v Kuhn,* 407 U.S. 258.
74. Flood with Carter, *The Way It Is.*
75. *The Sporting News,* July 8, 1972.
76. Flood with Carter, *The Way It Is.*
77. Flood with Carter, *The Way It Is.*
78. Flood with Carter, *The Way It Is.*

Chapter 5

1. Arnold Ramperstad, *Jackie Robinson: A Biography,* 1997.
2. Bill Beeck, *Veeck as in Wreck, the Autobiography of Bill Veeck,* with Ed Linn, 1962.

3. Author interview with Joe Brown, October 1994.
4. Mark Ribowsky, "Dave Parker Is the Closest Thing to Perfection," *Black Sports Magazine*.
5. "Dave Parker: 'The Ali' of Baseball's Diamond Ring," *Detroit Free Press*, October 11, 1979.
6. "Parker: Newest Link in Pirate Power Train," *The Sporting News*, August 2, 1975.
7. "Parker: Newest Link in Pirate Power Train.
8. *Cincinnati Post*, May 1, 1974.
9. Roy Blount, Jr., "Loudmouth and His Loud Bat," *Sports Illustrated*, April 9, 1979.
10. *Cincinnati Post*, May 1, 1974.
11. "Dave Parker: 'The Ali' of Baseball's Diamond Ring," *Detroit Free Press*, October 11, 1979.
12. Ribowsky, "Dave Parker Is the Closest Thing to Perfection."
13. Ribowsky, "Dave Parker Is the Closest Thing to Perfection."
14. "On the Lam with the Three Rivers Gang," *Sports Illustrated*, August 2, 1971.
15. Blount, Jr., "Loudmouth and His Loud Bat."
16. Al Oliver and Andrew O'Toole, *Baseball's Best Kept Secret: Al Oliver and His Time In Baseball*, 1997.
17. Blount, Jr., "Loudmouth and His Loud Bat."
18. Phil Musick, "I'm Pursuing the Ultimate," *Sport Magazine*, June 1979.
19. Marvin Miller, *A Whole Different Ball Game*, 1991.
20. Miller, *A Whole Different Ball Game*.
21. Miller, *A Whole Different Ball Game*.
22. Miller, *A Whole Different Ball Game*.
23. Miller, *A Whole Different Ball Game*; John Heylar, *Lords of the Realm: The Real History of Baseball*, 1994.
24. Heylar, *Lords of the Realm: The Real History of Baseball*.
25. Miller, *A Whole Different Ball Game*.
26. Miller, *A Whole Different Ball Game*.
27. Heylar, *Lords of the Realm: The Real History of Baseball*.
28. Miller, *A Whole Different Ball Game*.
29. Miller, *A Whole Different Ball Game*.
30. Miller, *A Whole Different Ball Game*.
31. Heylar, *Lords of the Realm: The Real History of Baseball*.
32. Miller, *A Whole Different Ball Game*.
33. Blount, Jr., "Loudmouth and His Loud Bat."
34. Blount, Jr., "Loudmouth and His Loud Bat."
35. Ribowsky, "Dave Parker Is the Closest Thing to Perfection."
36. Musick, "I'm Pursuing the Ultimate."
37. Blount, Jr., "Loudmouth and His Loud Bat."
38. Ralph Wiley, *Why Black People Tend to Shout: Cold Facts and Wry Views from a Black Man's World*, 1991.
39. "'Renegotiate' a Naughty Word," *The Sporting News*, September 8, 1977.
40. "'Renegotiate' a Naughty Word."
41. "'Renegotiate' a Naughty Word."
42. Ribowsky, "Dave Parker Is the Closest Thing to Perfection."
43. "Million Dollar Cobra Still Feels Bigotry's Bite," *Baseball Weekly*, August 17, 1993.
44. Dave Nightingale, "The Resurrection of Dave Parker," *The Sporting News*, March 1986.
45. Jim O'Brien, "'I'm the Best Player in Baseball,'" *Sport Magazine*, June 1981.
46. O'Brien, "'I'm the Best Player in Baseball.'"
47. "Parker Incident Mars Game," *The New York Times*, July 21, 1980.
48. "Parker Is Worth Every Penny to Reds," *The Sporting News*, August 22, 1985.

49. Musick, "I'm Pursuing the Ultimate."
50. "Ellis on Fan Shortage: Too Many Blacks," *Pittsburgh Post-Gazette*, June 5, 1975.
51. "Parker Accuses Media of Conducting Vendetta," *The Sporting News*, June 28, 1982.
52. "Parker Puts Pirates in Past, But He Knows How It Feels," *USA Today*, May 14, 1985.
53. O'Brien, "I'm the Best Player in Baseball."
54. O'Brien, "I'm the Best Player in Baseball."
55. "Parker and Fans Keep Testy Truce," *New York Times*, May 14, 1983.
56. Million Dollar Cobra Still Feels Bigotry's Bite."
57. O'Brien, "I'm the Best Player in Baseball."
58. O'Brien, "I'm the Best Player in Baseball."
59. *Associated Press*, September 12, 1983.
60. *Pittsburgh Press*, September 5, 1985.
61. *Pittsburgh Press*, September 5, 1985.
62. *Playboy*, September, 1979.
63. *Pittsburgh Post Gazette*, September 10, 1985.
64. *Pittsburgh Post Gazette*, September 12, 1985.
65. *Pittsburgh Post Gazette*, September 10, 1985.
66. *Pittsburgh Post Gazette*, September 13, 1985.
67. *Pittsburgh Press*, September 6, 1985.
68. *Pittsburgh Press*, September 7, 1985.
69. *Pittsburgh Post Gazette*, September 12, 1985.
70. *Pittsburgh Post Gazette*, September 12, 1985.
71. *Pittsburgh Post Gazette*, September 12, 1985.
72. *Pittsburgh Post Gazette*, September 12, 1985.
73. *Pittsburgh Press*, September 17, 1985.
74. *Pittsburgh Press*, September 20, 1985.
75. *The Sporting News*, March 24, 1986.
76. *The Sporting News*, March 24, 1986.
77. *The Sporting News*, March 24, 1986.
78. *Pittsburgh Post Gazette*, September 12, 1985.
79. *Pittsburgh Post Gazette*, September 12, 1985.
80. "Parker Trial Is 2-3 Years Away," *The Sporting News*, April 24, 1987.
81. "Parker Trial Is 2-3 Years Away," *The Sporting News*, April 24, 1987.
82. "Parker v Pirates $5 Million Can of Worms," *New York Post*, May 5, 1987.
83. *Albany Times Union*, December 12, 1988.
84. *Albany Times Union*, December 12, 1988.
85. "Million Dollar Cobra Still Feels Bigotry's Bite."
86. "Reds Sign Parker to Two-Year Pack," *USA Today*, December 8, 1983,
87. "Reds Sign Parker to Two Year Pack."
88. *The Sporting News*, March 24, 1986.
89. *The Sporting News*, December 2, 1985.
90. "Million Dollar Cobra Still Feels Bigotry's Bite."

Chapter 6

1. Mike Lupica, "Barry Bonds for President," *Esquire*, August 1, 1996.
2. "30/30 Vision," *Sports Illustrated*, June 25, 1990.
3. "30/30 Vision."
4. "30/30 Vision."
5. "Barry Bonds Striking Out on Own Path," *New York Post*, June 14, 1986.
6. "Barry Bonds Striking Out on Own Path."
7. "The Importance of Being Barry Bonds," *Sports Illustrated*, May 24, 1993.
8. "30/30 Vision."
9. *Baseball Weekly*, March 20, 1996.
10. "Paradoxical Bonds Reaches Pinnacle," *The Sporting News*, October 29, 1990.
11. "The Son Also Rises," *Inside Sports*, March 1991.
12. "Paradoxical Bonds Reaches Pinnacle."

13. "Paradoxical Bonds Reaches Pinnacle."
14. "The Son Also Rises."
15. "The Son Also Rises."
16. Peter Richmond, "Why Isn't Barry Bonds Willie Mays?" *Gentleman's Quarterly,* April 1994.
17. Richmond, "Why Isn't Barry Bonds Willie Mays?"
18. "I'm the Best Newspaper Seller in Baseball," *Sport Magazine,* March, 1992.
19. " I'm the Best Newspaper Seller in Baseball."
20. "The Superstar Nobody Knows," *Inside Sports,* October, 1996.
21. "The Superstar Nobody Knows."
22. "30/30 Vision."
23. "Bonds, New Owners Selling a Line," *USA Today,* December 8, 1992.
24. *The Sporting News,* October 29, 1990.
25. *Playboy,* July 1993.
26. "Barry Bonds, Too Little Too Late," *New York Times,* September 24, 1997.
27. "The Importance of Being Barry Bonds."
28. *Lupica,* "Barry Bonds for President."
29. Jerry Crasnick, "When in Doubt, Blame Someone Else," *Baseball America,* August 4-17, 1997.
30. Crasnick, "When in Doubt, Blame Someone Else."
31. "Bonds Drops Mask of Anger," *San Francisco Chronicle,* March 17, 1998.
32. *San Fransico Chronicle,* February 5, 1995.
33. *Nightline,* ABC TV, April 6, 1987.
34. Mike Bass, *Marge Schott: Unleashed!* 1993.
35. Bass, *Marge Schott: Unleashed!*
36. Bass, *Marge Schott: Unleashed!*
37. "The Silent Minorities," *Sports Illustrated,* April 5, 1993.
38. "The Silent Minorities."
39. "The Silent Minorities."
40. "The Silent Minorities."
41. "Selig Moves to Get Members of Minority Groups Into Decision Making Process," *New York Times,* April 25, 1999.
42. "Selig Moves to Get Members of Minority Groups Into Decision Making Process."
43. "Between the White Lines," *National Post,* October 18, 2000.
44. "Between the White Lines."
45. Jack R. Robinson, "*Baseball Has Done It,*" edited by Charles Dexter, 1964.
46. "Bonds on the Loose," *Baseball Weekly,* April 15, 1997.
47. Richmond, "Why Isn't Barry Bonds Willie Mays?"
48. "Bonds Drops the Mask of Anger."
49. "I'm the Best Newspaper Seller in Baseball."
50. "Bonds Drops the Mask of Anger."
51. "Bonds Is Best of HR Field," *Baseball Weekly,* July 16, 1996.
52. Lupica, "Barry Bonds for President."
53. Richmond, "Why Isn't Barry Bonds Willie Mays?"
54. "Is America Ready to Love Barry?" *Esquire,* June 11, 2001.
55. "Giant Sized Feat," *Washington Post,* July 15, 2001.
56. "While Sosa Exudes Pleasure, Bonds Perceived as Pain," *Washington Post,* August 8, 2001.
57. "He Love Himself Barry Much," *Sports Illustrated,* August 21, 2001.
58. "He Love Himself Barry Much."
59. "He Love Himself Barry Much."
60. Selena Roberts, "The Magic Is Missing as Bonds Approaches 70," *<publication/media>* September 26, 2001.
61. "Bonds Finally Finds Heart," *Chicago Sun-Times,* October 7, 2001.
62. "Giant Sized Feat."

Chapter 7

1. Jackie Robinson, *I Never Had It Made,* as told to Alfred Duckett, 1972.
2. "Baseball Accused of Racist Policies," Associated Press, November 15, 2001.
3. "Baseball Accused of Racist Policies."

4. "Between the White Lines," *National Post*, October 18, 2000.
5. "Clinton Statement on Curt Flood Act of 1998," US Newswire, October 27, 1998.
6. "Clinton Statement on Curt Flood Act of 1998."
7. "Clinton Statement on Curt Flood Act of 1998."

Bibliography

Several subject files from the National Baseball Hall of Fame Library were used in researching this book, including those for Rube Foster, Curt Flood, Dave Parker, and Barry Bonds.

Aaron, Henry, with Wheeler, Lonnie. *I Had a Hammer: The Hank Aaron Story*. New York: HarperCollins, 1991.

Abrams, Roger I. *Legal Bases: Baseball and the Law*. Philadelphia: Temple University Press, 1992.

Ackerman, Jan, and Remensky, Carl. "Hernandez: Over 40% Used Cocaine." *The Pittsburgh Post-Gazette*, September 7, 1985.

_____, and _____. "Parker: Buc Captains Gave Pills." *The Pittsburgh Post-Gazette*, September 13, 1985

_____, and _____. "Parker Used Cocaine for 3 Years." *The Pittsburgh Post-Gazette*, September 12, 1985

Adelson, Bruce. *Brushing Back Jim Crow: The Integration of Minor League Baseball in the American South*. Charlottesville: University of Virginia Press, 1999

Allen, Dick, with Whitaker, Tim. *Crash: The Life and Times of Dick Allen*. New York: Ticknor and Fields, 1989.

Anson, Adrian "Cap." *A Ball Player's Career*. Era Publishing, 1900.

Bankes, James. *The Pittsburgh Crawfords: The Lives and Times of Black Baseball's Most Exciting Team*. Dubuque, Iowa: Wm. C. Brown, 1991. Rev. ed., Jefferson, N.C.: McFarland, 2001.

Barber, Red. *1947: When All Hell Broke Loose*. New York: Doubleday, 1982.

Bass, Mike. *Marge Schott: Unleashed!* Sagamore Publishing, 1993.

Beaton, Rod. "Intensely Private Bonds Just Wants To Play Ball." *USA Today*, June 6, 1991.

Betzhold, Mike, and Casey, Ethan. *Queen of Diamonds: The Tiger Stadium Story*. West Bloomfield, Mich.: Altwerger and Mandel, 1992.

Blount, Roy. "Loudmouth and His Loud Bat." *Sports Illustrated*, April 9, 1979.

Bouton, Jim. *Ball Four: My Life and Hard Times Throwing the Knuckleball in the Big Leagues*. Edited by Leonard Shecter. New York: World, 1970.

Bruce, Janet. *The Kansas City Monarchs: Champions of Black Baseball*. Manhattan: University of Kansas Press, 1985.

Dixon, Phil, with Patrick J. Hannigan. *The Negro Leagues, 1867–1955: A Photographic History*. Mattatuck, N.Y.: American House, 1992.

Donavan, Richard. "The Fabulous Satchel Paige." *Collier's*, May 10–June 13, 1953.

Douglass, Frederick. *Narrative of the Life of an American Slave*. New York: Anchor Books, 1989.

Egan, Terry. "Similar But Not the Same, Larry Doby Was a Lesser Known Pioneer." *Dallas Morning News*, April 4, 1997.

Flood, Curt, with Carter, Richard. *The Way It Is*. New York: Trident, 1971.

Gregory, Robert. *Diz: Dizzy Dean and Baseball During the Great Depression*. New York: Viking, 1992.

Harrigan, Patrick J. *The Detroit Tigers: Club and Community 1945–1995*. Toronto and Buffalo: University of Toronto Press, 1997.

Heylar, John. *Lords of the Realm: The Real History of Baseball*. New York: Villard, 1994.

Hoffer, Richard. "The Importance of Being Barry Bonds." *Sports Illustrated*, May 24, 1993.

Holway, John. *Blackball Stars: Negro League Pioneers*. Westport, Conn.: Meckler, 1988.

_____. "Rube Foster: Father of the Black Game." *The Sporting News*, August 8, 1981.

_____. *Voices from the Great Black Baseball Leagues*. New York: Da Capo, 1992.

King, Martin Luther, Jr., *A Testament of Hope: The Essential Writings of Martin Luther King Jr.*, ed. by James M. Washington. New York: Harper and Row, 1986.

Koening, Bill. "As the First Black Player Larry Doby Endured No Less a Burden." *Baseball Weekly*, July 2, 1997.

Kuklick, Bruce. *To Everything a Season: Shibe Park and Urban Philadelphia 1909–1976*. Princeton, N.J.: Princeton University Press, 1991.

Locy, Toni, and Donovan, Dan. "1980 Big Year for Cocaine, Player Says." *The Pittsburgh Press*, September 5, 1985.

_____, and_____. "Received Pills from Stargell, Parker Says." *The Pittsburgh Press*, September 12, 1985.

_____, and _____. "Used Cocaine with Parker, Dodger Player Says." *The Pittsburgh Press*, September 7, 1985.

Lupica, Mike. "Barry Bonds for President: He May Not Be the Golden Child, But There's No Shame in His Game." *Esquire*, August 1, 1996.

Malcolm X. *Malcolm X Speaks*, ed. by George Breitman, New York: Grove, 1965.

Malloy, Jerry. "Rube Foster and Black Baseball." *Baseball in Chicago*. Cleveland, Ohio: SABR, 1986.

Miller, Marvin. *A Whole Different Ball Game: The Sport and Business of Baseball*. New York: Birch Lane, 1991.

Monroe, Al. "What Is the Matter with Baseball?" Newspaper clipping dated April 1932 from Rube Foster File, Hall of Fame Library, Cooperstown, N.Y.

Moore, Joseph Thomas. *Pride Against Prejudice: The Biography of Larry Doby*. New York: Harper and Row, 1984.

Musick, Phil. "I'm Pursuing the Ultimate...." *Sport*, June 1979.

Nightingale, Dave. "The Resurrection of Dave Parker." *The Sporting News*, March 4, 1986.

O'Brien, Jim. "I'm the Best Player in Baseball." *Sport*, June 6, 1981.

O'Day, Joe. "BB Warns: Flood Victory Kills Game." *Sunday News*, January 18, 1970.

Oliver, Al, with O'Toole, Andrew. *Baseball's Best Kept Secret: Al Oliver and His Time in Baseball*. Pittsburgh: City of Champions, 1997.

Paige, LeRoy "Satchel," as told to David Lipman. *Maybe I'll Pitch Forever: A Great Baseball Player Tells the Hilarious Story Behind the Legend*. Garden City, N.Y.: Doubleday, 1962.

_____, as told to Hal Lebovitz. *Pitchin' Man: Satchel Paige's Own Story* (1948). Reprint, Westport, Conn.: Meckler, 1992.

Peterson, Robert. *Only the Ball Was White: A History of the Legendary Black Players and All-Black Teams.* New York: McGraw-Hill, 1994.

_____. "Rube Foster: Best of the Black Managers." *Sport,* May 1975.

Polner, Murray. *Branch Rickey: A Biography.* New York: Atheneum, 1982.

Rampersad, Arnold. *Jackie Robinson: A Biography.* New York: Knopf, 1997.

Ribowsky, Mark. *A Complete History of the Negro Leagues, 1884–1955.* New York: Birch Lane, 1995.

_____. "Dave Parker Is the Closest Thing to Perfection." *Black Sport Magazine,* May, 1978.

_____. *Don't Look Back: Satchel Paige in the Shadows of Baseball.* New York: Simon and Schuster, 1994.

Richmond, Peter. "Why Isn't Barry Bonds Willie Mays?" *Gentleman's Quarterly,* April 1994.

Robinson, Frank, with Stainback, Barry. *Extra Innings.* New York: McGraw-Hill, 1988.

Robinson, Jackie. *Baseball Has Done It.* Edited by Charles Dexter. Philadelphia: Lippincott, 1964.

_____, as told to Alfred Duckett. *I Never Had It Made.* New York: G.P. Putnam, 1972.

"Rube Foster: Mastermind of Baseball Passes Away." *Chicago Defender,* December 13, 1930.

Ruck, Rob. *Kings of the Hill: Baseball's Forgotten Men.* Video. Produced by Rob Ruck and Molly Youngling. San Pedro Productions, 1993.

_____. *Sandlot Seasons: Sport in Black Pittsburgh.* Urbana: University of Illinois Press, 1987.

Stargell, Willie, with Bird, Tom. *Willie Stargell: An Autobiography.* New York: Harper and Row, 1984.

Tygiel, Jules. *Baseball's Great Experiment: Jackie Robinson and His Legacy.* New York: Oxford University Press, 1983.

Veeck, Bill, with Linn, Ed. *Veeck As in Wreck: The Autobiography of Bill Veeck.* New York: Simon and Schuster, 1989.

White, Sol. *Sol White's History of Colored Baseball, with Other Documents on the Early Black Game, 1886–1986.* Compiled and introduced by Jerry Malloy. Lincoln: University of Nebraska Press, 1995 (reprint).

Whiteside, Larry. "Doby Helped Open the Door Wider." 1987 World Series Program.

Wiley, Ralph. *Why Black People Tend to Shout: Cold Facts and Wry Views from a Black Man's World.* New York: Penguin Books, 1991.

Woodward, Bob, and Armstrong, Scott. *The Brethren: Inside the Supreme Court.* New York: Simon and Schuster, 1979.

Young, A.S. "Doc." "Rube Foster: Baseball's Negro Pioneer." *Hue Magazine,* August 1957.

Young, Dick. "Flood Plays, Short Pays." *The Sporting News,* April 29, 1971.

Young, Frank A. "Rube Foster: The Master Mind of Baseball." *Abbott's Monthly,* November 1930.

Zang, David W. *Fleet Walker's Divided Heart: The Life of Baseball's First Black Major Leaguer.* Lincoln: University of Nebraska Press, 1995.

Index